IMAGES OF WAR
FLYING LEGENDS OF WORLD WAR II

IMAGES OF WAR
FLYING LEGENDS OF WORLD WAR II

ARCHIVE AND COLOUR PHOTOGRAPHS OF FAMOUS ALLIED AIRCRAFT

PHILIP HANDLEMAN
with photographic contributions from
the portfolio of William B. Slate

Pen & Sword
AVIATION

First published in Great Britain in 2011 by
PEN & SWORD AVIATION
an imprint of
Pen & Sword Books Ltd,
47 Church Street, Barnsley,
South Yorkshire.
S70 2AS

ISBN 978-1-84884-308-0

A CIP catalogue record for this book is available
from the British Library

Typeset by Mac Style, Beverley, East Yorkshire
Printed and bound in India by Replika Press Pvt. Ltd.

Pen & Sword Books Ltd incorporates the imprints of
Pen & Sword Aviation, Pen & Sword Maritime,
Pen & Sword Military, Pen & Sword Select, Pen & Sword Military Classics,
Leo Cooper, Wharncliffe Local History

For a complete list of Pen & Sword titles please contact:
PEN & SWORD BOOKS LIMITED
47 Church Street, Barnsley, South Yorkshire, S70 2AS, England.
E-mail: enquiries@pen-and-sword.co.uk
Website: www.pen-and-sword.co.uk

Contents

Dedication

*To the courageous Allied airmen and ground crews of
World War II whose aircraft freed the skies*

and

*to the dedicated pilots and restorers who have
returned the flying legends to those skies*

Acknowledgements

Illustrated aviation book projects are often collaborative in nature and this one has been no exception. I am indebted to the following individuals and organizations, without whose assistance this book would not have been produced. As important as the various contributions were in completing the book, the responsibility for the final content is mine alone.

As mentioned elsewhere between these covers, the late William Slate's photographs represent an integral part of the book's visual core. I trust that the reproduction of Bill's images in these pages will serve as a fitting tribute to his expertise, skill and passion.

My old friend Jerry Rep of the Air Force Museum Foundation provided an especially desirable photograph with his usual cheerful good wishes. The archives of the National Museum of the US Air Force were a rich resource, as well.

Aviation sage and long-time colleague Walter Boyne, formerly of the Smithsonian Institution's National Air and Space Museum, came through with valuable images and, even more significantly, insightful tips. His wise counsel and earnest encouragement were, as always, deeply appreciated.

The ever diligent Jeffrey Rhodes of Lockheed Martin was most helpful in supplying archival photographs of some of his company's memorable World War II aircraft.

Both Robert Hanshew of the Naval Historical Center and Corey Black of the Naval Historical Foundation offered assistance in navigating the photographic reproduction services of their respective organizations. The result was assurance that the sometimes overlooked naval aircraft of World War II would be incorporated here.

The personnel of the Imperial War Museum's image licensing unit, including David Bell, were similarly helpful in steering me through what sometimes seemed a labyrinthine maze. I am grateful for the staff's patience as I delved into the IWM's impressive archives.

The 392nd Bomb Group Association strives admirably to preserve the history of a representative American bomber unit that operated from an English airfield during World War II. Through information and photographs posted on the association's website, it was possible to obtain insight into the milieu of wartime bomber operations.

Editor Peter Coles was understanding and supportive at every turn. His grasp of the dual disciplines of publishing and aviation is a rare commodity which has served to lift the end product to heights that would not otherwise have been attainable.

Above all, my thanks go to my wife Mary. She has embraced the many World War II flyers who have crossed our path, helping to elicit wonderful relationships that have augmented our knowledge and enriched our lives. Also, she is a championing voice when it matters most. How fortunate I am to have Mary as my wingman!

Author's Note

Well before his time, my late friend and fellow aviation enthusiast, William B. 'Bill' Slate, was summoned far beyond the stratospheric heights traversed by pilots on a typical day. A victim of amyotrophic lateral sclerosis, better known as ALS or Lou Gehrig's disease, Bill left an immutable void in the warbird world when he made his final ascent. On weekdays, he was an FAA air traffic controller, but on weekends during the air show season his time was spent in the joyous pursuit of photographing old military aircraft.

Bill's progression as an aviation photographer was abruptly curtailed just as his skills matured and his output blossomed. It is inexplicably unfair that in the prime of life a purposeful soul who embraced his passion would be denied consummation. How heartbreaking that someone who excelled at capturing high-performance aircraft in stop-action beauty, as if each machine racing past had been artfully posed, would lose the ability to hold his camera, much less focus it on his beloved subjects in the sky.

But my memories of Bill are laced with delightful vignettes from the air show circuit where, pressed between hordes of onlookers and the rope line, we craned our necks and squinted through viewfinders to get just the right camera angle. His favorite venue was the popular event known as the Tico Air Show, staged early in the season each year by the Valiant Air Command, a warplanes preservation organization in Titusville, Florida. The annual show is known for its outpouring of World War II-vintage aircraft and military planes of other eras.

At the first faint murmur of a Pratt's clattering or of a Merlin's hum in a distant corner of the sky, a smile lit up Bill's face. He tilted back, chin jutting up at the azure tapestry reliably punctuated with billowing white clouds in the heat of a Florida afternoon. When the classic plane finally roared into view, whether a shiny Texan trainer or a camouflaged Mustang fighter, the excitement was palpable. You heard the shutter curtain cycling furiously as Bill endeavoured to freeze the motion at the instant of framed perfection. The experiential thrill was turned into a photographic apotheosis. The compelling visual, recorded on film and printed on glossy paper in those days, could be savoured and shared later in the cool caverns of a big hangar.

It was obvious that Bill loved aircraft, especially the warbirds. At the air shows and fly-ins featuring restored World War II aircraft, his ardour was irrepressible and contagious. He never outgrew his childhood fascination for the piston-powered wonders and their magnificent flyers who ruled the skies in an earlier time. The daring fighter aces and heroic bomber pilots who flew these marvels to glory became legends and they inspired generations of youngsters. As an adolescent, Bill read about the wartime aerial exploits in magazines purchased for a dime a copy at the local drugstore and, as he grew older, it was only natural that he wanted to contribute his flattering pictures of the awesome flying machines to the current crop of aviation and adventure magazines.

A photographer, or for that matter any artist, who is at home with his or her subject matter stands a better chance of arriving at aesthetic fulfilment. Knowledgeable of and enthralled by the great aircraft of the late 1930s to the mid-1940s, Bill loved to walk the ramp at Tico and other hotbeds of warbird activity. Bill's intimate familiarity with the captivating lines of the legendary fighters and the muscular shapes of the venerable bombers served his photography well. When a sparkling warplane having just completed a comprehensive restoration zoomed along the flight line or joined up on the photo ship, Bill snapped away with his heart in every frame. It was not labour; it was adoration.

Thinking back to our times together, one of the endearing recollections I have is of Bill scrambling to board a rickety freighter aircraft that was shunned by aviation photographers of lesser fortitude. The ancient cargo ship had seen better days, but it was the only platform available at the time for aerial photo work, and Bill refused to let an opportunity pass that promised to carry him to a slice of the sky where there would be a radiant warbird within view and camera range.

Even on days that were a photographic washout because of a dreary overcast, Bill hopped onto whatever ride was offered to be there in proximity to the old warplanes. In a way, the picture-taking was secondary; it was the aircraft – the numbing reverberations, the pungent vapours, the high-pitched engine clamour, the beguiling rush of the heavy iron knifing through the sky – that drew him to that perch up above.

Though Bill is gone now, he has left a most enduring legacy. Not only do his many friends continue to reminisce, within earshot of thundering warplanes, about Bill's boundless enthusiasm, but the larger community of aviation aficionados now has the opportunity to gaze upon an array of fervidly snared photographs depicting the might and majesty of famous military aircraft. Each frame, in its uniqueness, speaks eloquently of the spirit of the warbird movement that so intrigued Bill. The selections from his portfolio are an extension of Bill himself. Fittingly, he lives on through the eye-popping aircraft pictures that follow.

Introduction

He was the quintessential stick-and-rudder man. That was my friend and frequent flying companion, Howard Ebersole.

When Howard did coordination exercises like Dutch-rolls and lazy-eights in my Stearman, I would glance at the turn-and-bank indicator in the rear cockpit where I sat. Invariably, the ball was centred throughout the seesawing motions of each manoeuvre as if an infallible robot were wielding the controls and ever so meticulously massaging the inputs. The consistency was remarkable because the aircraft's front cockpit, where Howard held sway, had no attitude instrumentation. I used to joke with him that his needle-and-ball was built-in, an imposing bionic component integral to his constitution.

Drawn to adventure in his early years, Howard sailed the Caribbean aboard a freighter. His knowledge of Morse code led to his employment as the ship's telegraph operator. One Sunday morning an urgent coded message was unscrambled in the captain's quarters. The old seaman, a southerner with a deep drawl, looked up from the deciphered scribbling and then gravely at his young telegraphy mate. 'Sparks,' the wizened sailor proclaimed, 'wez at waah!' As soon as the vessel docked, Howard ran to the nearest recruiting station and signed up for the Air Corps.

The dream of the young adventurer from the flatlands of Midwestern America had been answered. Howard was flying open-cockpit in helmet and goggles, silk scarf and leather jacket, soon to be adorned with the vaunted silver wings of the mightiest air power organization the world had ever seen. From the first day when his instructor swung the control stick around without warning, such that it battered the poor cadet's knee caps, his infatuation with flight blossomed into a fully fledged love affair. The imperiousness of officialdom was a small price to pay for the privilege of soaring aloft in high-performance aircraft.

Howard was assigned to bombers during World War II, and some of his missions were historic for their impact on the course of the war. Targets included Magdeburg, Kiel, Wilhelmshaven, and even Berlin. Howard participated in all of these missions. Yet, when asked which was his most memorable, he said it was the low-level supply mission over the German town of Wesel as part of the big Allied push known as Operation *Varsity* in the war's waning days.

It was supposed to be a milk run. Bundles of supplies were to be dropped to the troops who had crossed the Rhine the night before. When Howard, the deputy lead pilot, reached the drop zone, flak filled the sky. He watched helplessly as a B-24 from another bomb group cart-wheeled into the ground. Also, C-47 tugs and troop-carrying gliders littered the landscape, some still smouldering from fire they had taken during the prior day's assault.

Howard belonged to the 578th Bomb Squadron of the 392nd Bomb Group. The group was known as the 'Crusaders' and the group emblem played off that theme (which by today's standards would be considered so politically incorrect as to be unthinkable). The emblem depicted a knight in body armour and a tasselled helmet, clutching a heavy lance in one hand and a cross-laden shield in the other hand while riding a bomb on a downward trajectory. In retrospect, the emblem is almost comical for Howard was the last person in the world to harbour any classical crusading inclinations; he was, like his compatriots, an American flyboy, not a religious zealot.

The symbol of a crusading knight was simply meant to convey the 392nd's unwavering determination to vanquish tyranny so that people everywhere could be free to think, act, speak and pray as they pleased. In filling the cockpits and cabins of their bombers with such motivation, Howard and the group's other airmen differentiated themselves from most victors in the long history of warfare. These flyers, members of what has popularly become known as the Greatest Generation, were not conquerors, but they were, as the official nickname of their aircraft proclaimed, liberators. The group emblem was sewn into Howard's leather jacket and worn at the beginning of a vocation in service to his country and the cause of freedom.

Late in his life, after accumulating more than 12,000 flight hours in a long and distinguished military and civilian flying career, Howard and I moseyed through the capacious display areas of the National Museum of the US Air Force. Etching a mark on a scratch pad every time we passed a type he had piloted, we tallied up the count at day's end. The total came to twenty-eight types.

In a gallery of wood-and-fabric designs mixed with the earliest all-metal configurations, there were the obligatory trainers, first flown as a student, and later in some cases as an instructor. Then, in a corner flanked by familiar shapes, there was the big bomber in which, as a young man barely beyond his teens, he pressed on to targets amid blankets of fire. Soon after we came upon the early jets, in one of which he earned the enduring gratitude of his squadron mates for having saved the life of his wingman. In the middle galleries, there were the pointy-nosed and delta-winged jets in which he pioneered the métier of guided missiles. Lastly, there were the light transports used to shuttle generals.

The disparate aircraft were connected by a trio of threads woven by this quiet and unassuming man whose character manifested a yen for the sky, a penchant for the camaraderie of men at arms, and a commitment to the warrior ethos. One autumn day, he left the confines of the quaint airport near our homes for a trip abroad. Nearly a half-century since his deployment to foreign shores as a newly minted flying officer, he joined a small cadre of his surviving bomb group teammates to revisit the place where, with youthful exuberance, they had staked their claim as world-changing aviators.

On what was reported to be a typically 'damp, cool, and misty morning' reminiscent of the days when the 392nd Bomb Group formed up for long and harrowing missions over central Europe, Howard and his buddies gathered at the Eighth Air Force's old Wendling Airfield, nestled in the back country of Norfolk in East Anglia, to dedicate a refurbished memorial to their 747 cohorts who did not make it home alive and to the base's entire wartime roster. Much like the mythical post-war Archbury air base in the definitive World War II bomber movie *Twelve O'clock High*, Wendling had deteriorated into a fragment of its glorious past.

Most structures, including the control tower, had disappeared while the balance of the wartime buildings had been converted to sustainable, if pedestrian, uses. The officers' club, once the social hub for lonely airmen far from home, was transformed into an auto parts warehouse. The runway that had launched the group's Consolidated B-24 Liberators on 285 combat missions appeared derelict, a victim of time's inexorable ravages. Strewn across its remnants were large rectangular buildings of a turkey farming business.

What mattered, though, on that blustery morning of Saturday, 7 October 1989 were the memories of those thirty veterans who came to honour their fallen comrades. Under the American flag that waved briskly in the breeze and enveloped in the warm graces of the local townspeople, the aged warriors paid their respects. There were speeches that attested to the faithfulness of all who had served at Wendling. A wreath was laid at the memorial's pedestal. Then a minute of silence followed that left everyone in tears.

The next day dawned uncharacteristically sunny. Howard and his fellow veterans went to the American Military Cemetery at Madingley near Cambridge to offer a tribute to their colleagues who rest there. Again, the American flag fluttered in the wind. However, this day the stars and stripes were cast against the brilliant sun. The verse of John McCrae inscribed at the base of the flagpole held especial import for the visiting veterans. Surely, the poet had these men and their silenced comrades in mind when he wrote, '... To you from failing hands we throw the torch – Be yours to hold it high.'

Still shrouded in morning shade to the east, across the reflecting pools with their borders of polyantha roses, the majestic Wall of the Missing could be seen. Formed from English Portland limestone, the wall contains 5,125 names of American servicemen never recovered or identified. Of these, 115 served alongside Howard in the 392nd.

Getting closer, the lettering became readable, the names familiar. Engraved atop the wall and within view of the 3,812 neatly aligned white headstones that define the cemetery's emerald grounds is an excerpt from a testimonial by Howard's most senior wartime leader, indeed, the supreme Allied commander in the final push to liberate Europe.

At the wall's dedication, Dwight Eisenhower praised those who had sacrificed 'to defend human liberty and rights.' He spoke these words fittingly in St Paul's Cathedral in London. (Miraculously, during the relentless aerial blitz of London, with bombs exploding all around, St Paul's escaped unscathed, a symbol of the free world's determination to hold on for a better tomorrow.)

The engraving in homage to those consecrated by the wall continues, 'All who shall hereafter live in freedom will be here reminded that to these men and their comrades we owe a debt to be paid with grateful remembrance and the high resolve that the cause for which they died shall live eternally.'

About a decade after Howard's trip to Wendling, he signed an album of personal anecdotes and candid snapshots that had been privately published by a memorial association devoted to preserving the history of the 392nd. On a page with a picture of one of his group's B-24s approaching to land at Wendling Airfield, Howard inked a note of thanks to my wife, Mary, and I for our friendship and then added, 'Enjoy these stories. In them you will meet some real American heroes. I am proud to have known and flown with many of them.'

In turn, I am proud to have known and flown with Howard.

Howard Ebersole was the quintessential stick-and-rudder man. In a military flying career that spanned several wars, both hot and cold, he retained his love for his country and of flying.

Though only in his early twenties, First Lieutenant Howard Ebersole was an aircraft commander in the 578th Bomb Squadron, 392nd Bomb Group, which operated out of the Eighth Air Force's Wendling Airfield in East Anglia, England, from August 1943 until the end of the European war in May 1945. This was a typical formation of the 392nd's Consolidated B-24 Liberators as they pressed the daylight bombing campaign against targets in Germany.

Chapter 1

Keep Them Flying

Salutes

From spring through autumn, at out-of-the-way airports scattered across both the American and European landscapes, aviation enthusiasts can be observed tinkering with the machines that warm their hearts and light their souls.

At the crack of dawn, when the air is still and the morning dew glistens, a distinctive shape, sleek yet strapping, emerges from the rows of weather-beaten hangars. In the glow of the brightening sunrise, the silvery ship projects a simple majesty, and even the uninitiated perceive that this is not just any aircraft but a rare breed with a story as profound and scintillating as the sky itself.

A deep-bellowed rumble accompanied by a spurt of grey-white smoke signals the first stirrings amid the sleepy surroundings. The old warhorse, cajoled by her proud and adoring master, brays and whinnies. An ornery temperament is the apparent price for such refined pedigree. Gentle stroking of the throttle brings fits and starts until the myriad moving parts harmonize. Once bridled, the bronco purrs.

There is a purposeful veer off the taxiway onto the adjoining open pasture, flat grassland being the preferred surface for antiques of wartime vintage. A serpentine path to the grass runway reflects the lack of forward visibility from the pilot's angled perch. With the old-style configuration that places the third wheel in the tail, this ship requires special handling on the ground; she isn't for novices.

The fuselage's exposure sideways reveals classic star-in-bar markings to passersby on the contiguous country lane. Though weekend chores loom, some of the motorists slow to a stop on the side of the road. They know this aircraft is different than the everyday spam cans that crisscross the sky. Yes, this one is of grandpa's time, the kind he flew when he served during World War II. Or maybe an uncle crewed on the type. Or perhaps a distant relative, whose exact role during the war has been lost to time, happened to serve contemporaneously with this mare and her stable mates.

From the corner of his eye, the pilot catches a glimpse of the roadside gawkers. A few of them brave the morning chill and stand by their cars, zipping up their jackets and rubbing their hands. Others twist their necks in the warmth of their cars. One in the disparate assemblage waves to the aircraft and soon everyone clustered along the road follows.

The morning's flight has turned, innocently enough, into an impromptu flying display. That's the way it should be, the pilot muses. He tips his head in acknowledgement and raises his arm in a swooping motion over his head to the extent his harness permits. Before swivelling the tail around to point the ship's nose into the wind for the pre-flight run-up, in the universal language of aviation he flashes a determined upraised thumb to his spontaneous roadside audience.

The engine howls and the ship vibrates. Toe brakes are stressed to their limit. There is a trace of an easing up, just for a fleeting moment. The sequence repeats itself. The magneto checks verify that sparks are ablaze to keep the cylinders firing. Another falloff, this one more pronounced than the prior two, followed by the engine's return to a full-throated roar, signals that the propeller governor is cycling through pitch settings okay.

Performing the last checklist item, each control surface travels full-throw in a symmetrical wagging of elevator, rudder, and ailerons. For a person unschooled in the conventions of flying, the aviator's ritual might seem like clownish antics or perhaps an exotic attempt at communication, like a naval officer transmitting a coded message by resolutely gesticulating with signal flags. Alas, there is no message from the aircraft's control surfaces' proportionate swings to-and-fro and back-and-forth except that the ship is ready for launch.

A hush falls over the road where now traffic has choked to a virtual crawl and the whole fence line is occupied by a row of cars parked bumper to bumper. Sensing that the take-off is about to occur, a father lifts his toddler over his shoulders to enable a better view. The aircraft inches ever so methodically down the wide-berthed path carved out of what once was a cornfield, the prop wash spraying the latent moisture into a hazy plume much as a speedboat cleaves a trail of white-capped wake in its passage through a similarly malleable medium.

In the cockpit, all gauges are on the redline. The propeller blades whirl furiously and the tip rotation is so brisk that a 'whomp-whomp-whomp' drumbeat throbs in rapid staccato. It's a mesmerizing sensation that does not reach the field's perimeter for another second because of the distance from runway to road. When the wave hits the onlookers, it is like a tsunami. The air suddenly is thick with the ear-splitting clatter and the ground undulates from the unrestrained power of the mighty warplane rising into its domain, destined to rejoin ghosts of a noble past.

The little boy straddled atop his dad's shoulders absorbs the initial burst, the awe, the bluster, and the bravado thrown off by the accelerating ship as it races across the resplendent field. Just then, without any prompting but surely with the benefit of tales handed down through the generations bolstered by weekend afternoons taking in classic flying films, the young chap raises his right arm, crosses his forehead with his hand, all fingers outstretched and touching, and then throws the straightened hand out and drops it premeditatedly down. A salute.

Unrehearsed, simple, and genuine, the gesture is a generational tribute as pure and as fitting as operators of the restored warplanes ever receive. And, with experiences like this, such testimonials pass on through the flyable machines to those who first flew them into glory. It is also a symbol of how the movement to keep World War II aircraft in the air has informed and touched those of subsequent generations.

The ship leaps off the turf and holds steady no more than half a wingspan above the deck. Landing gear legs fold into the wing and the ship picks up steam as its speed over the runway builds tangibly. Nearing the far end of the field, the big, burly contrivance is transformed into a slim, shiny dart suddenly pointed skyward.

Strain on the airframe is perceptible, but when the machine was riveted together by women nicknamed 'Rosie', it was stressed for several lifetimes of such high G-force manoeuvres. Indeed, this specimen survived action in the world's greatest armed conflict and has gone on to outlive its successors which have long since been consigned to static displays at aviation museums or to gate guard duty at air bases. To be sure, maintenance is intensive on this relic, yet its longevity is virtually assured by the indefatigability of the volunteer teams that delight in polishing every inch of their charge until its skin is brought to a blinding sparkle.

Barely within sight, the dot in the distant sky arcs gracefully to one side in a reversal of direction and glides back down to where the climb started, etching a huge teardrop against the crystalline expanse. By now, any townsfolk who slept in have been wakened; it is all right to have a gentle night's slumber broken by the triumphal thunder of one of the boisterous wonders that long ago, against incredible odds, calmed a chaotic planet about to slip into a calamitous abyss.

A cry goes out from someone in the crowd at the fence. 'Here it comes! Here it comes! It's making a pass!'

As if tying up a loose end, the aircraft hurtles back over its outbound track. Again low to the ground, it approaches like a sprinting hotrod on a cushion of air. The beauty comes into full-frame for those lucky enough to be carrying a camera of some sort.

The slightest dip is followed by a measured pull-up and then the streamlined husk heaves over on its wing tip in knife-edge. At full-throttle, the ship is cross-controlled in extremis, not really flying but pushing forward on momentum and looking as if suspended in limbo. For a split second the mass of ingeniously formed aluminium is frozen with the overhead planform in crisp outline, the wing spread perpendicularly in a mocking rejoinder to the physical laws of flight. Remarkably, it's possible to read the fuel grade, printed in simple block letters near the mid-wing fuel caps. If this instant lasted for an implausible country minute, a sharp-eyed bystander could count the rivets dotting the metal structure.

In the morning's most piercing roar, the aircraft levels and shoots for a higher stratum. It shrieks over the heads of the gathered devotees. Then, in a flash, it is lost again to roam in the boundless sky, the inviting realm that is its natural habitat. There is no way for the pilot to know, but the people watching below break out in sustained applause and loud cheers.

An old gent who arrived late to the roadside show, exits the back of his family's utility vehicle. The aircraft has already vanished, but the man, assisted by members of his family, at first leans against the vehicle for support and then makes a point of righting himself apart from any crutch or helping hand. Standing erect, he peers in the direction that the aircraft was last seen and his face, marked by wrinkled jowls and a furrowed brow, exudes an unremitting pride as though he was one of the originals who rode astride the mighty warbird long before the morning's gallivanting.

Like the boy before, the old-timer forms a salute, only in this case it bears the attributes of someone who has rendered the honour a thousand times. Not perfunctorily but conscientiously, even emphatically, he elevates his arm and brings it back down ever so stiffly, deliberately, feelingly. His gaze won't leave the sky. His eyes, blurred over by tears welling up inside, speak of fighting the good fight, camaraderie among men of the air, and flights possessed of immortality.

When the warbird pilot returns from his invigorating jaunt, the crowd will be gone. Yet the impressions made and the memories kindled will live on for a long time to come, fostering a keen appreciation for those who served in the cause of freedom and instilling a dream of infinite possibilities in which even the sky is no limit. By soaring into the exalted heights of the illimitable kingdom where the aircraft's rich legacy was fashioned years ago, the warbird's pilot, supported by a fervent volunteer community, serves to elevate us all.

The Movement

Chino, Oshkosh, Midland, Duxford and many lesser known villages and hamlets have something in common. These outposts punctuating the wide open countryside are the nerve centres of a vibrant movement driven by spirited believers. The common thread uniting the adherents is a commitment to not merely preserve the aircraft that filled the roiling skies during World War II, but to maintain their airworthiness.

It has become extraordinarily expensive to operate the old warplanes. Also, the supply is dwindling because of unavoidable attrition. At the same time, the demand for these historic antiques has risen astronomically as they are rightly perceived to be irreplaceable. Where once it was possible to pick up a war surplus Merlin-powered fighter like the revered North American Aviation P-51 Mustang for a relative pittance, today there are no bargains and anyone in the market for such hardware will have to spend upwards of a million-and-a-half dollars for a restoration of the calibre that has become *de rigueur* for the era's iconic aircraft.

The extravagant purchase price is not the only aspect reflective of the high costs involved in the warbird world. Equally as daunting are the operational expenses. The skyrocketing costs of fuel, oil, maintenance, insurance and hangar rental all coalesce to make ownership prohibitive. Not surprisingly, in recent times there has been a proliferation of air museums and flying foundations which pool the resources of many supporters. This is especially the case when it comes to operating such big wartime aircraft as the Boeing B-17 Flying Fortress. It is implausible that anyone could operate one of these four-engine bombers without the army of volunteers available to a fully fledged aviation museum.

Much of the restoration work goes on behind the scenes. Fitting push-pull tubes, adjusting the tension of flying wires, and replacing shock absorber seals don't constitute the glamorous stuff of aviation lore, but they are essential to keeping the antiques in the air. Those who labour in the corners of dimly lit and draughty hangars with hands soaked in grease and coveralls stained by spills of hydraulic fluid are the true unsung heroes of the warbird movement.

Without the devotion of these skilled enthusiasts to the cause of returning the historic aircraft to their bailiwick, there would be only pretty but motionless artefacts anchored to the ground accumulating dust, subservient to the omnipotence of gravity. At designated times each year most of the established institutions with a stable of flyable warbirds stage breathtaking exhibitions of their collections. The annual air shows and fly-ins are stimulating, even rejuvenating events, and all the more so when the hangar doors are swung open and the colourful assortments are trotted out.

The highly publicized affairs are usually well attended for they are excellent opportunities to observe some of the most famous aircraft ever built in rip-roaring routines, not only one by one but whole formations at once. The organizers arrange for the re-enactment of flying experiences of World War II as they unfolded at the time. Indeed, the Commemorative Air Force, which has been a leading warbird organization since its founding in Texas in 1957, has prided itself on offering a dramatic show at its home airport in Midland that includes pyrotechnic-laced re-enactments of major air battles, starting with the surprise Japanese attack on Pearl Harbor.

In an amazing marshalling of resources, the flying display typically comprises a vast number of Zero, Kate, and Val replicas. They dive down at stage centre, trailing plumes of smoke, an air raid siren whines and explosives are detonated on the ground to simulate the real thing. A few American fighters are scrambled and a squirrel-cage pattern sprouts against the afternoon's cumulus build-up. Before long, the defending fighters chase the foreign attackers in mock dogfights. By some accounts, it's a corny act, but no one can deny that this is a slice of history reborn – no matter how mawkish the narration and predictable the outcome.

Throughout the next few hours, the restored aircraft, representing all theatres of combat during World War II, are simply magnificent. Every detail has been addressed, right down to the number and alignment of victory marks painted on the nose of an ace's aircraft. Old photos are used for reference and if the legendary pilot is still alive, he is consulted.

In the days leading up to the big event, the 100 or so vintage aircraft scheduled to participate in the show are 'gussied up'. Spit and polish are evident for when the crowds fill the ramp and form along the flight line; the trainers, fighters, bombers, and transports appear immaculate, surely better even than when they first rolled off the assembly line. Now, instead of being instruments of war expected to dive into battle, they are prized possessions to be celebrated.

When these aircraft were used for their intended purpose, appearances were, of course, quite secondary; it was all about performing the mission back then. By contrast, as collector's items now, the warbirds are lovingly wiped down after every flight. The maintainers are serious about the care that the rare aircraft receive. There is a pervasive cognizance that each remaining ship is a treasure, in some cases the sole remaining airworthy example. The prevailing mindset says: If anything happens to bring the ship to grief, it won't be for lack of attention by the ground crews.

Each year since 1970, large segments of the aviation world have congregated in tiny Oshkosh, Wisconsin, in mid-summer for what is widely regarded as the granddaddy of fly-ins. The town's population, which hovers year-round at just 50,000, jumps during the week of the annual event to more than seven times that number. For the duration of the gathering, the usually quiet airport remains the busiest in the world.

Warbirds of every variety occupy an enormous swath of the grassy meadow on the north-west side of Wittman Airport's main north/south runway. With the concerted planning of a superb staff and the invaluable hands-on involvement of dozens of loyal volunteers, the vintage military aircraft are aligned in neat rows according to type.

Since about 350 of the North American Aviation AT-6/SNJ Texan advanced trainers are still listed in the FAA registry, there are more of these aircraft on the grounds than any other type from the World War II era. The Texans, and their Canadian cousins – the Harvards – stretch for as far as the eye can see. When these ships take to the sky during their portion of the much-admired warbird flying displays, their mass formations represent the largest such aerial assemblages of the advanced trainers since they last flew in actual military service.

The Oshkosh-based Experimental Aircraft Association believes so strongly in the preservation of historic warplanes that it offers membership in a subgroup expressly dedicated to the task. Known as Warbirds of America, its members are drawn from the movement's diehards. During the year, they preen their historic aircraft in preparation for the annual event in Oshkosh, which goes by the name AirVenture.

At the fly-in, experts in fields like metalwork, fabric, welding, control systems, etc. review the aircraft whose owners wish to have their objects of affection judged in the restoration competitions. The restorers' obsession with perfection can be so pronounced that the judges are beside themselves. Standards are so high that it is a unique form of veneration to be honoured by the EAA. Afterwards, wherever the award-winning warbird goes, the EAA's appellation follows it.

Indicative of the zeal to have a great-looking antique gracing the AirVenture show line, many of the owners and their family members jump out of their aircraft upon parking in the warbird section and promptly begin squirting cleanser on the oil-splattered cowl using spray bottles they packed for the trip. Wing leading edges and landing gear struts get the same treatment so that within minutes of arrival an aircraft that has journeyed all the way from the prairies or the sawgrass country is looking pristine.

The enthusiasm for a glittering ship is contagious. In every direction, the field brims with examples of brilliant antiques, which form a refulgent vista of blues, yellows, greens and browns. The air is rich in the sweet aroma known to pilots that blends the effluents of burnt avgas and oil. All the senses are immersed in the feast that commemorates some of the greatest aircraft that have ever touched the sky and the heroes who flourished in them.

Of course, the main accruement is the brotherhood among like-minded souls, the shared experiences and the bonding that comes from a collective belief and a common pursuit. The culmination is AirVenture. This is where the faithful congregate. This is where the gathered warbird enthusiasts take to flight. The equipping, readying and burnishing at home during the rest of the year are but a prelude to Oshkosh.

Through its network of chapters (which the organization refers to as 'squadrons'), the Warbirds of America keeps the flame burning at home throughout the year. Pilots and mechanics can compare notes with their fellow members. When a vexing maintenance issue arises or a hard-to-find part needs to be located, the owner of a rare old ship is not alone. A member in the chapter has probably encountered the same issue and will happily offer a solution, sometimes lending a specially sized socket wrench to complete the job.

Where a huddle forms amid the rows of warbirds during AirVenture's weeklong celebration, you know that there is a paladin of the air at the hub, an ace perhaps. Reverent flyers and their curious children solicit informational tidbits from the aged luminary. What was it like duelling over Rabaul or helping the breakout from Bastogne? The answers are never timid. It's as if the man with the leathery face and hearing impairment who is at the centre of attention, like his few remaining comrades at arms, is prepared still to clamber into the cockpit and throttle forward should the order come.

Against the din of the busy airport, the followers lean forward and hang on every utterance. After all, this is not just an eminently skilled pilot, but an exemplary patriot. His moments of truth, while dangling alone and under attack, were infused with repeated surges of personal courage. His airmanship was important, but he evinced something on top of that. An extra measure of determination stared down the danger. A mindset that said 'I'm in this for all or nothing' reigned over the cockpit such that the warrior riding at the tip of the spear aimed to accomplish the mission no matter what.

Whole battles, and thus, whole wars, hinge on individual acts of bravery. Without the aged heroes spotted every so often roaming the grounds at events like AirVenture, the world would have devolved into a desolate place.

What an honour for warbird pilots to reintroduce the ever-dwindling number of distinguished World War II veterans to their former aircraft types, in some cases to the very ships they flew to glory. Taking them along to rise again into the vacuum of open sky where they had carved out a victory that unshackled much of the world from the clutches of oppression is the ultimate high, a reward that exceeds quantification. And when the last of the Allied aviators of World War II is gone, there will be reminders of the record of valour for in some corners of the wild blue yonder the period's warplanes will be seen and heard, the undying guardians of a remarkable heritage.

That is why today's warbird enthusiasts pledge to keep them flying.

Chapter 2

Taming the Sky: Trainers

In the lead-up to World War II, young men aspiring to be pilots were generally exposed to flight in the light-powered, enclosed-cockpit aircraft of the Civilian Pilot Training Program. But, once their military flying training began, they were treated to the open-cockpit experience. Invariably, those initial hops were tinged with more than a little trepidation. Once the 'willies' were overcome, the fledgling aviators got down to the serious business of learning to master the aircraft in its myriad attitudes around the three axes.

Intense concentration on developing the requisite skills left scant time to enjoy the exhilaration of flight. Yet, when the era's high-time military pilots reflect on their many hours aloft, the fondest memories are often of solo flights in their trusty trainers. This was the purest of flying – the wind whistling through the bracing wires and a silk scarf flapping in the slipstream during weaves to and fro in ever more coordinated lazy-eights.

At the outset of America's involvement in the war, draft-age citizens perceived aviation as an electrifying endeavour, a field that evoked dreams of daring and adventure. Throughout the 1930s, the National Air Races stoked the public's fascination with flight. One-of-a-kind aircraft decorated in flashy colours and flown by swashbuckling pilots like the inimitable Roscoe Turner set speed records in hair-raising competitions, which aroused a staunch air-mindedness. Pulp magazines like *Air Stories* and *Flying Aces* and weekend matinees like the Errol Flynn classic *Dive Bomber* romanticized the life of military aviators.

Many of the wartime enlistees had immersed themselves in the popular aviation literature so that they came into the service with basic knowledge. The principles of flight, the forces acting on a wing, the cycles of a reciprocating engine, etc. were often already comprehended by the budding flyers as their ground school courses unfolded. Of great importance, too, was real-world experience that came from tinkering with mechanical things, especially the innards of automobiles.

Arguably, American youth, more than any other segment of the world's would-be pilots, possessed the formidable advantage of hands-on experience replacing flat tyres, changing oil, adjusting carburettors, and performing other maintenance and repairs on the family car or their own jalopy. Knowing such vehicular systems enhanced their ability to understand analogous aircraft systems and eased their interface with the training planes.

Cadets were subjected to a regimented life in usually utilitarian surroundings where classroom lectures and study time consumed much of the day and night. The prospect of eventually flying in military aircraft was a strong incentive to keep one's nose to the grindstone. When that moment came, donning parachute and the other paraphernalia of flight for the first excursion into the air, cadets were awed, scared, and tickled all at once.

The initial foray into the sky was normally more of an orientation flight rather than an instructional flight. The cadet got to take a deep breath and relax, at least in relative terms, while the instructor let his student 'feel' the aircraft and familiarize himself with the local geography. It was the introductory step in a carefully orchestrated programme that proceeded in phases with milestones along the way.

Nothing would ever compare with the maiden solo flight. Emphasis on honing skills followed. Rolls, loops, spirals, stalls, and spins were part of the primary syllabus. By the time cadets moved on to the next phase they had a solid understanding of the rudiments of flight.

Years of national ill-preparedness had to be rectified in short order. There was a rush to get the cadets qualified and off to battle. Accordingly, if a trainee did not measure up in the allotted time, he was scheduled for a dreaded check ride to be administered by a seasoned pilot, almost always a military officer rather than a civilian instructor under contract.

Dreams of admittance to the rarefied pantheon of aces could come crashing down in a heartbeat. The time it would have taken to coach a lagging student who might otherwise have made a good military pilot just was not available in the context of an ongoing war. Some of those who washed out of flight school went on to become navigators, bombardiers, and on-board gunners. Each contributed greatly to mission success.

From learning the fundamentals of airmanship in open-cockpit monoplanes like the Fairchild PT-19 Cornell and Ryan PT-22 Recruit or biplanes like the Boeing PT-17/N2S Kaydet/Yellow Peril and Naval Aircraft Factory N3N (also known as Yellow Peril), the cadets progressed to the intermediate phase and after that to the advanced phase. Wisely, the US Army and Navy used virtually identical platforms in these two phases, the Vultee BT-13/SNV Valiant basic trainer and the North American Aviation AT-6/SNJ Texan advanced trainer.

At the end of the gruelling process, Army Air Forces' silver wings and US Navy gold wings were pinned onto the uniforms of newly minted second lieutenants and ensigns, respectively, signifying the fruition of a hard-earned personal achievement. For the country, it meant that distant skies would fill soon with an armada of warplanes wielded by competent airmen, committed and able to subdue the forces of malevolence and emancipate the multitudes yearning for the blessings of freedom.

Pilot Preparer: Boeing Stearman PT-17/N2S Kaydet/Yellow Peril

Perceiving the need for significantly more trainer aircraft during the lead-up to American involvement in World War II, the US military increased procurement of such planes in the late 1930s and then steeply ramped up their acquisition once America officially entered the conflict. Among the military's several primary trainer types of the time was the two-seat, open-cockpit biplane built by Boeing's Stearman Aircraft unit in Wichita, Kansas. Famed designer/entrepreneur Lloyd Stearman had long since sold his stake in the company that he had founded in 1927 and that had borne his name, but Boeing refined one of the company's pre-existing designs as its entry in the military's primary trainer competition.

By 1939, the evolved type was known internally as the Model 75. The fuselage had a tubular-steel frame mostly covered with cotton linen fabric. The wings consisted of wood ribs and spars which were also fabric-covered. A variety of engines were mounted on the aircraft, the two most common being the seven-cylinder Continental R-670 and the nine-cylinder Lycoming R-680, both of which were rated in the 220-horsepower class. A total of 10,000 of

The Boeing Stearman was America's leading primary trainer of World War II. It was a demanding and effective trainer. This is a US Navy N2S-3 in March 1941.

these aircraft were produced, making the type the most prevalent American primary trainer during the war.

Both the US Army and Navy operated the type. Aircraft designation depended on which service operated the aircraft and which engine was installed. For example, the Army version with the Lycoming was the PT-13 and the Army version with the Continental was the PT-17. The Navy's equivalents were the N2S-5 and N2S-3, respectively. Slight variations in instrumentation and airframe resulted in a wide range of additional designations, the most notable being the PT-27, which included a cockpit canopy for cold-weather flying.

Early on, the Army's trainers had yellow wings and a blue fuselage, but in April 1942 this colour arrangement was superseded by an all-silver finish. By contrast, the US Navy had adopted an all-yellow scheme. The aircraft's official nickname was Kaydet. But, because of the Navy's colour preference, the Navy version was sometimes called the Yellow Peril (as was the all-yellow N3N biplane trainer produced by the Naval Aircraft Factory). However, the Boeing trainer was usually referred to simply as the Stearman. Interestingly, that name continues in popular use to the present, a lasting tribute to the predecessor company and its founder.

The Stearman excelled at conveying the basics of airmanship. In the air it was a straightforward machine, though somewhat underpowered given its weight and drag. Ground handling and landings were challenging because of the lack of forward visibility and the closely coupled landing gear. It was capable of garden variety aerobatics and served as a valuable stepping stone to the more complex aircraft to be encountered next in the training programme.

After the war, many Stearman trainers were employed as agricultural applicators. Others were sold to foreign governments. Most remaining examples have been restored either in authentic military colours or in eye-catching air show schemes. Outfitted with more powerful engines, smoke systems, and control surface modifications, some appear on the air show circuit doing low-level aerobatics and performing with wing-walkers.

Specifications
Manufacturer: Boeing
Type: two-seat primary trainer
Powerplant: one 220-horsepower Continental R-670 radial piston engine
Wingspan: 32 ft 2 in
Length: 25 ft 0 in
Height: 9 ft 2 in
Maximum take-off weight: 2,950 lb
Maximum speed: 124 miles per hour
Cruising speed: 95 miles per hour
Service ceiling: 13,300 ft
Range: 300 miles

The Boeing Stearman was a primary trainer for both the US Army and US Navy during World War II. Pictured in flight is a Navy N2S-5 near the Naval Air Station at Patuxent River, Maryland, in 1943.

Pilot Teacher: Vultee BT-13/SNV Valiant

Vultee's basic trainer evolved from a design concept that was a harbinger of things to come in the aviation industry. The idea was to build common parts and assemblies that would be interchangeable for four separate but similar types of aircraft, each with a different and distinct mission. Certain critical components would change in the production process as needed for completion of each of the four types, but the main structure would remain the same.

The pre-war Army was drawn to the basic combat trainer type more than the other three proposed types. However, as conceived, this Vultee design employed retractable landing gear and a 600-horsepower engine. These were considered extravagant features for what would be an intermediate trainer, so Vultee toned down its proposed trainer. With fixed landing gear and a 450-horsepower engine, the Army ordered 300 of these aircraft, newly designated the BT-13, in September 1939.

The BT-13A had a different version of the Pratt & Whitney Wasp Junior engine than the original model. Later, the aircraft was changed with the installation of a 24-volt electrical system, which led to it being re-designated the BT-13B. The US Navy followed the Army with a significant purchase in August 1940. The Navy's versions were designated SNV-1 and SNV-2, these being equivalent to the Army's A and B models, respectively.

Because the type's production was so substantial and hurried, engine production was not able to keep up. The Wright Whirlwind filled the void. Aircraft with these engines were designated the BT-15. In total, a whopping 11,537 Valiants were built up to 1944, far exceeding the Vultee company's initial expectations for any of the types in its unorthodox concept.

The Valiant was a success in imparting instrument flying skills and smoothing the way to the advanced trainer. The greenhouse-style canopy provided some shielding from the elements, but the aircraft was known as a noisemaker because of the shrill thumping given off by the propeller blade tips. However, it was not the noise but the shaking when stalled that caused the aircraft to be known unofficially as the Vibrator.

Specifications
Manufacturer: Vultee
Type: two-seat basic trainer
Powerplant: one 450-horsepower Pratt & Whitney R-985 Wasp Junior radial piston engine
Wingspan: 42 ft 0 in
Length: 28 ft 10 in
Height: 11 ft 6 in
Maximum take-off weight: 4,496 lb
Maximum speed: 180 miles per hour
Cruising speed: 140 miles per hour
Service ceiling: 21,650 ft
Range: 725 miles

Pilot Maker: North American AT-6/SNJ Texan

What many consider the premier training aircraft of all time started as an internally funded project at North American Aviation's predecessor company in the mid-1930s. Known as the NA-16, the prototype performed on a par with combat aircraft of the time. The fixed-gear, two-seat, enclosed-cockpit, low-wing monoplane impressed Army evaluators to the point that several dozen of these were ordered with the basic trainer designation of BT-9.

The US Navy soon followed with its own order, replacing the BT-9's original 400-horsepower Wright R-975 with the 500-horsepower Pratt & Whitney R-1340. Under the US Navy's designation system, the trainer was the NJ-1. The basic trainer ultimately to emerge from the BT-9 programme was the BT-14, which had a 450-horsepower Pratt & Whitney R-985. The Royal Canadian Air Force operated the type, which it called the Yale.

In 1937, when the Army Air Corps opened a competition for what it dubbed a basic combat trainer, North American already had the makings of a great design to fit the bill. Using the NA-16/BT-9 as the basis for its entry, it added a more powerful engine and retractable landing gear. The concept was accepted and became known as the BC-1.

The Army changed its designation from basic combat trainer to advanced trainer, and at that point the aircraft's designation became AT-6. (A few years after the war, all trainers were given the prefix 'T', which shortened the type's designation to T-6.) The aircraft, nicknamed the Texan, became the Army's advanced trainer just as huge numbers of student pilots were entering the flying program to meet wartime demand. The US Navy bought large quantities of the type with the designation SNJ. The Canadian version was called the Harvard.

The old adage that an aircraft that looks good will fly good certainly applies in the case of the Texan/Harvard family of trainers. Performance was zestful and on-board systems were complex, yet the aircraft was neither too speedy nor too abstruse to befuddle adept and

The AT-6/SNJ Texan was an outstanding advanced trainer. It was generally acknowledged that if a cadet could master the Texan he could fly just about anything in the US military's aviation inventory. This is a Navy SNJ-5. Note the dirigible in the background.

diligent cadets. In fact, the trainer had good handling characteristics. It required a surprisingly light touch in rolling manoeuvres given its heft.

With a variable-pitch propeller, wing flaps, a radio, navigation equipment, retractable landing gear, and 600 horses under the cowl, the AT-6/SNJ gave the would-be aviator much to digest. If the cadet could master this aircraft, it was felt that he could fly anything in the military's inventory. The cockpit layout, general performance and overall feel were fitting preparation for the many fighter types rolling off the assembly lines during the war. For good reason, this trainer was called the Pilot Maker.

The most numerous models were the Army's AT-6C and AT-6D with more than 3,000 and 3,400 built, respectively. The AT-6/SNJ series had an international reach, as well. This was not simply because many British and Canadian student pilots received training in the type. It is estimated that over time the type was exported to or built under licence in eighty-three countries.

An astounding 17,000 aircraft in the Texan/Harvard trainer series were produced. The trainer made an enormous contribution to the war effort. Having the right aircraft at the right time and in adequate numbers helped to make victory possible. Flying veterans of the time often remark that they loved their experience in the Texan.

Reflecting the utility of the type, after the war the AT-6/SNJ continued to be used as a military trainer in the US and abroad. Also, the aircraft found a combat role. Notably, during the Korean War specially modified variants were employed as forward air controllers. Today, Texans are frequently seen at air shows, often in formation teams which delight in titillating audiences by pulling high-G manoeuvres with engines cranked at full throttle and props revved to the maximum.

Specifications
Manufacturer: North American Aviation
Type: two-seat advanced trainer
Powerplant: one 600-horsepower Pratt & Whitney R-1340 Wasp radial piston engine
Wingspan: 42 ft 0 in
Length: 29 ft 6 in
Height: 11 ft 9 in
Maximum take-off weight: 5,300 lb
Maximum speed: 205 miles per hour
Cruising speed: 170 miles per hour
Service ceiling: 21,500 ft
Range: 750 miles

Chapter 3

Commanding the Sky: Fighters

Fighter pilots have always personified the flying mystique. From air warfare's first plane-to-plane duel, those who have tussled in the naked air have never failed to capture the public's imagination. Analogous to the gunslingers of the Old West or the gladiators of ancient Rome, the audacious personalities who have manoeuvred wildly aloft in life-and-death contests against equally eager and confident foes are, in some observers' view, imbued with an extra measure of steeliness in their DNA.

In the modern age, for the moment at least, dogfighting has all but vanished. In large part, this is because air-to-air combat has evolved into such a technologically driven science with the US so dominant in the latter twentieth century and early twenty-first century that the victor is determinable *a priori*. By contrast, in World War II air combat outcomes were predicated mainly on inexact and variable human factors much like in Manfred von Richthofen's time. The pilot's eyesight, locomotor skills, airmanship and fighting spirit heavily influenced the end result. Air fighting was more an art, a craft, a set of skills handed down by masters through apprenticeships and honed by experience in the crucible of spine-tingling skirmishes in the three-dimensional battle space.

Tactics and sometimes teamwork added invaluably to the equation. Also, depending on the nature of the match-ups between opposing pilots, the aircraft itself could make the difference. Any technical advantage offered by the underlying platform or its many subsystems was most welcomed by the on-board occupant whose success, and longevity, hung in the balance.

Old-time fighter pilots craved manoeuvrability. Out turning the opponent was commonly the key to winning. Speed, especially in a climb or dive, was desirable for alternately engaging when opportunity knocked or disengaging at unpropitious moments, when discretion warranted, to come back and fight another day. Powerful and reliable armament enhanced lethality. Protective features like self-sealing fuel tanks and armour plating provided a measure of confidence.

Of course, each design feature came laden with trade-offs. More guns meant more weight; a fatter wing to hold more fuel produced an increase in drag, and so on. During the inter-war years, significant progress in aeronautics and powerplant development occurred such that by the eve of World War II the main belligerents had impressive aircraft either already in operational squadrons or on the drawing boards awaiting production.

In America, anti-interventionist sentiment impeded military aircraft production, but it did not hold back advances in aviation technology nor did it diminish the enthusiasm of the country's remarkable engineering talent pool. The attack on Pearl Harbor prompted an instant reversal in the national outlook with unreserved approval for a program to mass produce tens of thousands of military aircraft each year. In a sign of unprecedented industrial prowess, the 'arsenal of democracy' began churning out whole fleets of fighters from factories with legendary names like Curtiss, Grumman, Lockheed, North American, Republic and Vought.

Even more amazing, teams at these and other icons of design and manufacturing innovation rapidly and continually modified airframes to operate more effectively in faraway combat zones, taking into account conditions in the field and counter-developments applied to front-line aircraft of the Axis powers. Similarly, the great engine makers like Pratt & Whitney in the US and Rolls-Royce in Britain further refined their stalwart radial and inline models, respectively, so that performance metrics like horsepower ratings continued to rise throughout the war. Clearly, the imperatives of global conflict fostered incredible headway in record time.

When the best airframes were mated with the best engines, the result was a mighty war machine. Standouts included the P-51 Mustang, the F4U Corsair, and the P-47 Thunderbolt. By war's end, the piston-powered aircraft had reached its apex and a novel kind of propellerless aircraft, powered by an entirely new propulsive technology – the jet engine – came on the scene, poised to revolutionize the future of air warfare and flight in general.

Fork-Tailed Devil: Lockheed P-38 Lightning

When it first appeared, the distinctively configured P-38 turned heads. From time to time, doubts arose about this groundbreaking design. But throughout its wartime service, the Lightning accumulated an impressive record that included being the first US fighter to shoot down a German aircraft and the mount of more than 100 aces in the Pacific theatre.

Gestation of the type started when alarm over the emerging Nazi threat caused the US Army Air Corps to reverse years of passivity in fighter development by fostering modern designs. In February 1937, proposals were sought for both a single-engine and a twin-engine fighter. Lockheed submitted concepts for the latter.

Lockheed's project design team was headed by the company's chief designer, Hall M. Hibbard. An important presence on the team was a rising young engineering impresario, Clarence L. 'Kelly' Johnson. The company's engineers envisioned a high-altitude interceptor that would control the airspace from a perch well above accepted operating altitudes of the time.

Key to achieving the altitude advantage would be the use of superchargers to compress the thin air at high altitudes which, in turn, would provide the necessary engine power. Engine exhaust was used to drive a turbine, which resulted in turbo-superchargers, initially the General Electric B-1. The Allison engine was chosen because of its availability and adaptability.

Other design innovations included a twin-boom layout. The propellers turned in opposite directions to negate torque effect, the tendency of a propeller's gyroscopic motion to pull an aircraft away from the chosen flight path. This feature meant that the fighter would be an unusually stable gun platform. The centre nacelle accommodated the lone pilot in a bubble canopy, affording unobstructed in-flight visibility in all quadrants. A concentrated battery of guns was housed in the nacelle's otherwise hollow nose. Another distinction was tricycle landing gear.

The P-38 was so fast that when pushed into a power dive it ran into the then mysterious phenomenon of compressibility whereby a shockwave builds up on the airframe's leading

An unconventional design, the Lockheed Lightning featured a twin-boom configuration which enabled the firepower to be clustered in the otherwise empty nose nacelle. The most common armament was one 20-mm cannon and four 0.5-in machine guns.

edges nearing the speed of sound. The problem was solved by reshaping the wing fairing at the root and installing a dive brake. In any case, some pilots who flew the type in Europe retained doubts. The seven P-38 fighter groups that operated in the European theatre tallied an overall kill-loss ratio that was roughly even.

Differences in the operational environment helped Lightnings to excel in the Pacific theatre. The type's most highly publicized mission was the shooting down of Admiral Isoroku Yamamoto on 18 April 1943. In an amazing feat of long-distance navigation, P-38s arrived at the interception point at just the right time. The debate continues as to which pilot scored the kill, but subsequent review has led many to believe that it was Lieutenant Rex Barber rather than the initial claimant, Captain Tom Lanphier.

In dogfights, Japanese Zeros had the turn advantage, but P-38s were faster. Also, Japanese aircraft generally were fragile in construction and thus prone to break-up if hit by the Lightnings' withering firepower. Indeed, America's highest scoring aces were P-38 pilots of the Pacific theatre, Major Richard Bong of 5th Fighter Command with forty kills and Major Tom McGuire of the 475th Fighter Group with thirty-eight kills.

The Lightning proved to be versatile. Variants included the so-called 'Droop Snoot' which was designed to accommodate a bombardier in a glazed nose. There were reconnaissance models, designated F-4 and F-5, in which the nose was crammed with cameras. At war's end, the P-38M was to be a night fighter with a radar operator in a back seat reading signals gathered by a radar antenna located in a nose-mounted pod. As a testament to its combat prowess, a total of 10,038 Lightnings were built throughout the war.

Specifications (for P-38L)
Manufacturer: Lockheed
Type: single-seat fighter
Powerplant: two 1,600-horsepower Allison V-1710-111/113 inline piston engines
Wingspan: 52 ft 0 in
Length: 37 ft 10 in
Height: 9 ft 10 in
Maximum take-off weight: 21,600 lb
Maximum speed: 414 miles per hour
Cruising speed: 290 miles per hour
Service ceiling: 44,000 ft
Range: 450 miles normal, 2,260 miles maximum
Armament: one nose-mounted 20-mm Hispano cannon and four nose-mounted 0.5-in machine guns, up to two 1,600-lb bombs or ten rockets

Tank Buster: Bell P-39 Airacobra

The P-39 represented a radical departure in fighter design when it first flew as an experimental platform on 6 April 1938. The aircraft's engine was located behind the pilot, which raised concerns about the location of the centre of gravity. Also, the fighter was given tricycle landing gear, a rarity at the time.

On the plus side, engine placement freed much of the nose so that it could house an unusually large weapon in the cavity, the heavy 37-mm T-9 cannon. The cannon's barrel

This simulation of a night attack dramatically captures the full fury of the Bell P-39 Airacobra's guns blazing away. The 37-mm cannon barrel protruding through the spinner was the centrepiece of the aircraft's armament. Machine guns in this model were located in the fuselage decking behind the nose and in the wings.

protruded through the aircraft's spinner. The inline Allison engine drove the propeller by an extension shaft, which ran directly under the pilot.

The aircraft's weight-and-balance was nonstandard such that when the Airacobra went into a spin it required lots of altitude to recover. Army pilots were instructed to bale out if a spin occurred less than 10,000 feet above the surface. The unforgiving handling characteristics did not endear the aircraft to its early operators.

As often happens in the developmental stage, the P-39's weight increased due to various design imperatives. Also, the turbo-supercharger which had been installed in the first model was abandoned. The lack of the turbo-supercharger, combined with the added weight, reduced speed.

Airacobras entered service with the RAF's No. 601 Squadron in September 1941, but the aircraft's performance did not meet expectations. The theoretical air-to-air combat attributes simply did not pan out in real-world use. These aircraft were hastily withdrawn.

The P-39 served respectably in US Army Air Corps units in the Pacific, notably out of Port Moresby, New Guinea, and in North Africa. The aircraft found its niche in Soviet hands. The large forward-firing cannon was ideal for ground attack, especially against heavily armoured German tanks. The Soviets also managed to successfully utilize the Airacobra as an air-to-air fighter in the low and medium altitudes.

Almost all of the 2,095 P-39N models went to the Soviet Union. Another large contingent to the Soviets consisted of the P-39Q, which was the most numerous model in the aircraft's production run. Nearly half of all P-39s ended up in Soviet service. The type flew on the Eastern front. P-39s increasingly hampered German forces as the air fighting initiative shifted in the Allies' favour.

In the final analysis, the P-39 was not an aircraft for all seasons, but a capable machine when it came to certain kinds of missions. Some of the P-39's design features did not catch on. For example, the side doors providing pilot ingress/egress never supplanted moving canopies.

Despite a number of drawbacks, there were positives like the main firing track being directly in line with the pilot. Also, the P-39's cockpit was comfortable and afforded good visibility in all directions. By war's end, 9,558 Airacobras had been produced.

Specifications (for P-39Q)
Manufacturer: Bell Aircraft
Type: single-seat fighter
Powerplant: one 1,200-horsepower Allison V-1710-83 liquid-cooled V-12 piston engine
Wingspan: 34 ft 0 in
Length: 30 ft 2 in
Height: 11 ft 10 in
Maximum take-off weight: 8,400 lb
Maximum speed: 386 miles per hour
Cruising speed: 200 miles per hour
Service ceiling: 36,000 ft
Range: 650 miles
Armament: one 37-mm cannon firing through propeller hub, two fuselage-mounted 0.5-in machine guns, two 0.3-in machine guns in wing pods, one 500-lb bomb

Bird of Prey: Curtiss P-40 Warhawk

Dating back to the 1920s through much of the 1930s, the Curtiss-Wright Corporation's fighters were among the top-notch frontline aircraft in the US Army inventory. The company's family of open-cockpit, biplane Hawk fighters is regarded as one of the all-time classic fighter series, noted for its simple yet elegant design aesthetic. In 1935, the company attempted to redefine its position as a leader among fighter design shops by developing a metal, low-wing, cantilevered monoplane with a big-barrelled air-cooled engine.

Designated the P-36, in general outline this aircraft was not unlike other fighters being proposed or even some of the successful racing planes of the time. Despite the attempt to leap into the next generation, the design represented only an incremental transformation. In October 1938, the aircraft was refitted with an inline liquid-cooled engine and re-designated the XP-40.

Some of the Army's early production models of the P-40 were stationed in the Philippines when the Japanese attacked in December 1941, but their numbers were not adequate to provide a meaningful defence. The RAF took delivery of 110 P-40Bs, which in British service were known as Tomahawks. Most of these were dispatched to North Africa where they achieved mixed results, ultimately being relegated to the ground support role.

In 1941, predating America's official entry into the war, 100 P-40Bs destined for the RAF were sent instead to the Far East for service with the American Volunteer Group (AVG), popularly known as the Flying Tigers. These aircraft were painted with shark's teeth on their noses. Pictures of the AVG planes in Chinese Nationalist colours with the sinister nose markings took on an iconic status. Interestingly, this artwork was copied from that which appeared on British Tomahawks in North Africa. In an ironic twist, the RAF had adopted the nose art that had been emblazoned on *Luftwaffe* fighters.

AVG commander Claire Chennault knew that the Japanese fighters could climb faster and higher than the Tomahawks as well as outmanoeuvre them. But he also knew that his P-40s had their own set of attributes including fast diving capability and meaningful firepower. If the right tactics could be applied, the P-40s would inflict damage and come out on top in the looming air battles. He counselled the AVG pilots to avoid traditional dogfighting and instead make a single pass followed by a clean break. The technique worked and by later historical analysis the group's kill/loss ratio was determined to be at least ten to one.

The P-40C had additional armour and self-sealing fuel tanks, but performance suffered with the extra weight. A more powerful version of the Allison engine was installed in the P-40D, which changed the aircraft's outward appearance. The British nicknamed this model the Kittyhawk. A bomb-carrying capability came with the P-40E. By late 1943, all the upgrades that were possible to squeeze the last bit of performance out of the design culminated in the P-40N. This was the definitive variant of the American Warhawk. More than 5,000 units of this model were built.

The P-40 was virtually obsolete at the outbreak of the war, yet its availability in a time of dire need led to the production of a whopping 16,802. Given the abundant numbers, various models of the P-40 saw action as front-line combat aircraft for the Army Air Forces in most theatres of the war. About a quarter of them were contracted for by Britain and roughly half of those were diverted to the Soviet Union.

Although it was burdened by an outdated design, it managed to rack up a worthy record. With the recognition that the type was outclassed by more modern fighters, Warhawks finally stopped rolling off the assembly line in September 1944.

The P-40 traced its lineage back to the alluring Curtiss Hawks like the P-6E of the 1920s. This early model P-40 belongs to the 20th Pursuit Group. In 1940, while based at March Field in California, the unit became the second in the Army Air Corps to fly the type. Note the candy-stripe pattern on the rudder, a feature regularly applied to pre-war Army aircraft.

Specifications (for P-40N)
Manufacturer: Curtiss-Wright
Type: single-seat fighter/bomber
Powerplant: one 1,300-horsepower Allison V-1710-81 inline piston engine
Wingspan: 37 ft 4 in
Length: 33 ft 4 in
Height: 12 ft 4 in
Maximum take-off weight: 8,850 lb
Maximum speed: 378 miles per hour
Cruising speed: 290 miles per hour
Service ceiling: 38,000 ft
Range: 240 miles
Armament: six 0.5-in machine guns, one 500-lb bomb

Jug: Republic P-47 Thunderbolt

The highly regarded P-47 Thunderbolt had its origins in the air power zeal of Alexander de Seversky and the design genius of Alexander Kartveli. Under the Seversky corporate banner, Kartveli devised a big-barrelled, all-metal configuration that employed a powerful radial engine and retractable landing gear. The Army Air Corps was duly impressed and ordered an initial batch in 1936 with the designation P-35.

In 1938, famed aviator Jacqueline Cochran flew one of these Thunderbolt precursors to victory in the cross-country Bendix Trophy race, streaking from Burbank, California, to Cleveland, Ohio, in slightly more than eight hours. However, the world of aeronautical design was advancing quickly with war on the horizon and the Seversky fighter was being eclipsed by newer aircraft. Kartveli essentially refined his design, working for Republic Aviation which had absorbed the Seversky operation in October 1939.

The fighter that emerged was the P-43 Lancer. It was more streamlined and had an engine with a higher horsepower rating. This aircraft bore the look of the great aircraft to come. On 12 June 1940, Kartveli submitted his masterful design to the Army Air Corps. He opted to stick with his general concept that the brute power of a big but simple air-cooled radial engine would compensate for the concomitant increase in drag. The centrepiece was a turbo-supercharged 18-cylinder monster of an engine.

A gigantic four-bladed propeller required uncommonly long and sturdy landing gear legs. For all the bulk, the payback came in the amount of armament that could be carried. The resulting P-47, officially nicknamed the Thunderbolt, had four 0.5-in machine guns staggered in each wing. Plus, the aircraft could sling up to 2,500 pounds of ordnance under its wings.

Often referred to as the Jug (appropriately derived from 'juggernaut' and accentuated by the aircraft's jug-like shape), this fighter was in some ways an anomaly. Pre-war design theory suggested that small fighters made the most sense. Kartveli gambled that just the opposite – a hulking airframe – would work if sufficiently powered. There were teething problems which were to be expected since the design was cut from an inimitable mould. But the inherent possibilities overshadowed the early glitches.

In 1942, the 56th Fighter Group received the P-47B, the type's first production model. By April of the following year, the 56th was flying bomber escort missions as part of the Eighth Air Force in England. The 56th became the highest-scoring group within the Army Air Forces during World War II.

An aircraft weight and balance problem was resolved by repositioning the engine almost a full foot forward of its prior location. This and other modifications, like a belly attachment point for either a bomb or an expendable fuel tank, resulted in the P-47C. The ultimate model was the P-47D, which had an improved engine, more armour, expanded weapons carriage, and (from the -25 production block) a bubble canopy replacing the razorback arrangement.

The Thunderbolt shined as an escort fighter once the centreline fuel tank was added to extend the aircraft's range. Although it was not the most agile fighter given its considerable weight and mammoth proportions, those features helped it to absorb otherwise catastrophic damage from enemy fighters and antiaircraft artillery. The fighter's ability to withstand punishment and return its occupant to base was much appreciated by the front-line pilots.

It should be noted that the aircraft enjoyed a fast diving speed which it could use to attack Messerschmitt Bf 109s and Focke-Wulf Fw 190s from above or, alternatively, to escape from those more manoeuvrable fighters. Another exemplary facet of the P-47's service was its prowess in ground attack. Here, again, its heft made it ideal for the mission.

The last of the line was the P-47N, a significantly reworked model notable for its longer wingspan and greater fuel capacity. It was conceived for the Pacific theatre of operations where long, over-water flights were the challenge by late in the war. Production of all models of this outstanding fighter totalled 15,683.

Specifications (for P-47D)
Manufacturer: Republic Aviation
Type: single-seat fighter/bomber
Powerplant: one 2,535-horsepower Pratt & Whitney R-2800-59W Double Wasp engine
Wingspan: 40 ft 9 in
Length: 36 ft 2 in
Height: 14 ft 8 in
Maximum take-off weight: 17,500 lb
Maximum speed: 433 miles per hour
Cruising speed: 350 miles per hour
Service ceiling: 41,000 ft
Range: 1,900 miles maximum (with three drop tanks)
Armament: eight 0.5-in Browning machine guns, up to 2,500 lb in bombs or ten rockets

Thoroughbred: North American P-51 Mustang
In early 1940, with the Battle of Britain about to unfold in the skies over the British homeland, the British Purchasing Commission visited America in search of desperately needed fighters. The Commission's attention was drawn to Curtiss which had a long history of producing sleek fighters and which was on the cusp of churning out its latest, the P-40. At the same time, in discussion with North American about the possibility of the company building additional P-40s under licence from Curtiss, North American's president James H. 'Dutch' Kindelberger proffered a design concept which he said would outperform the P-40 even though it would use the same Allison engine.

Impressed by the proposal, on 10 April the Commission gave the company a mere 120 days to deliver a flying prototype. This was a breathtaking demonstration of faith given that North American's only experience in building fighters was with the ill-fated P-64, a rather staid radial-engine machine of which only six were built for export. Kindelberger relied on a couple of extraordinarily talented designers, Raymond H. Rice and Edgar Schmued, whose design was destined to profoundly impact the coming air war and for ever enliven the chronicles of aviation history.

The design incorporated advanced features. A laminar-flow wing was used, the first for a production aircraft. With symmetrical upper and lower aerofoil surfaces and the point of thickest camber set back cordwise, better high-speed performance would be attainable. Also, the coolant radiator was located in the lower aft fuselage to minimize drag. A major innovation was an aerodynamic duct system with an adjustable air scoop in the belly to efficiently route airflow for cooling purposes.

The Republic P-47 Thunderbolt was a bear of a fighter. Its unofficial nickname of Jug was an abbreviation of juggernaut.

Three days ahead of the tight deadline, the airframe was ready. However, Allison wasn't able to spare an engine just then. It took a few months more for the engine to arrive. The maiden flight of the new aircraft, designated NA-73X, occurred on 26 October 1940, an amazing 186 days after the parties agreed to proceed. In keeping with the company's projections, the Mustang, as the fighter would be called, achieved a speed in level flight at altitude that was 25 miles per hour faster than that of the P-40.

The British had already placed orders and the Americans followed a bit later, designating the fighter the P-51. The RAF Mustangs' initial combat mission was flown on 27 July 1942. Real-world performance wasn't quite up to snuff because of the 1,150-horsepower Allison V-1710-39 engine. The Mk I and Mk IA versions of the Mustang were relegated to ground attack and reconnaissance roles. Then the idea to replace the Allison with the Rolls-Royce Merlin took hold. In both Britain and the US, flight tests were arranged.

With the installation of the 1,520-horsepower Merlin 60-series engine built under licence by Packard, the fighter performed like never before, reaching a sizzling speed of nearly 440 miles per hour. This mating of the American airframe with the British engine was a magnificent union. By most appraisals, from that point forward the Mustang was the war's greatest all-around fighter.

North American Aviation P-51 Mustangs are seen here en masse with propellers turning, readying to taxi out for take-off. The alternating white and black stripes were ordered by General Dwight Eisenhower who wanted to ensure that Allied aircraft involved in the D-Day invasion would not be mistaken for enemy aircraft and possibly subjected to friendly fire.

The Mustang is best known for its service in the European theatre, but the type was also used in the Pacific theatre. In a dramatic pose, a ground crewman signals all is clear to a P-51D departing an improvised airstrip on the captured island of Iwo Jima. Note the steel planking which was laid down as an impromptu runway to expedite flight operations.

The US Army had earlier ordered Allison-powered versions, designated P-51 and P-51A. There was a brief interlude in which a dive-bomber version was ordered, designated the A-36. This model was identical to the P-51A except for the addition of dive brakes. The first US model powered by the Merlin was the P-51B. This model was built at North American's Inglewood, California, plant. Demand required that production occur at another company plant, this one in Dallas, Texas. The fighters built there had the designation P-51C. All models up to this point had aft canopy sections that were flush with the upper fuselage frame.

The ultimate iteration of the Mustang was the P-51D. This model brought all the advantages together in a sterling platform. It had a bubble canopy for a clear view in all directions and a dorsal fin to improve stability. Six wing-mounted 0.5-in machine guns concentrated devastating firepower on targets within the pilot's sights. Later D models were outfitted with an 85-gallon fuel tank behind the pilot's seat which, on top of the 184-gallon capacity in the wing tanks, enabled longer escort missions. It was also possible to attach 110-gallon drop tanks.

As an escort fighter, it excelled in protecting Eighth Air Force and Fifteenth Air Force bombers on long-range missions, including those that reached all the way to Berlin. Notably, the 332nd Fighter Group, comprising the famed Tuskegee Airmen, did an outstanding job safeguarding B-17s and B-24s in their P-51Ds, even knocking down *Luftwaffe* Me 262s in some of the early encounters with the menacing jet interceptors.

Because the P-51D was such a superb air-to-air fighter, it helped the Allies achieve air superiority, which hastened the end of the European war. Among the many aces who flew the type was the colourful commander of the Eighth Air Force's 4th Fighter Group, Lieutenant Colonel Donald L. Blakeslee.

Other Mustang models were produced, including the P-51K, which was like the P-51D, except that it had a troublesome propeller, and the lightweight P-51H, which went into action in the Pacific late in the war. Total Mustang production, including some built overseas under licence, was 15,586. Re-designated the F-51, the fighter was used to great effect by the US Air Force in Korea.

Specifications (for P-51D)
Manufacturer: North American Aviation
Type: single-seat fighter
Powerplant: one 1,590-horsepower Packard V-1650-7 (Merlin) liquid-cooled V-12 piston engine
Wingspan: 37 ft 1 in
Length: 32 ft 3 in
Height: 13 ft 8 in
Maximum take-off weight: 11,600 lb
Maximum speed: 448 miles per hour
Cruising speed: 362 miles per hour
Service ceiling: 41,900 ft
Range: 1,300 miles
Armament: six 0.5-in Browning machine guns, two 500-lb bombs, or eight rockets

Innovative Newcomer: Bell P-59 Airacomet

Chief of the Army Air Forces Henry H. 'Hap' Arnold believed strongly in adopting the latest technologies for the war effort. Unfortunately, when America entered the war, its aircraft were few in number and generally antiquated. The US had to play catch-up and often faced the choice between promising but risky new hardware and passé designs that were readily available. Starting in the 1930s, both the British and the Germans had pursued a revolutionary propulsive technology, the jet engine, led by Frank Whittle and Hans von Ohain, respectively.

The US military was remiss in recognizing the value of the jet engine, but while Arnold visited Britain in April 1941 he saw the experimental Gloster E-28/39 jet aircraft. He quickly tasked Bell Aircraft to develop America's first jet plane. The programme was steeped in secrecy from the outset.

For security purposes, Bell used the XP-59 designation that had been assigned to its discontinued twin-boom, piston-powered pusher fighter. When its jet prototype reached southern California's Muroc Dry Lake (now Edwards Air Force Base) in autumn 1942, it was fitted with a mock propeller to give the appearance of a conventional aircraft. The jet was nicknamed the Airacomet. It was a tricycle-gear, mid-wing monoplane with a raised empennage to accommodate the turbojets' exhaust.

The first American military pilot to fly a jet aircraft was Bill Craigie in the Bell P-59 Airacomet at Muroc Dry Lake (now Edwards Air Force Base) in October 1942. The aircraft was sluggish and simply not suited for combat, but it was a first step for the US Army Air Forces into the jet age.

A graceful in-flight appearance was exuded by the P-59B. This model was equipped with nose-mounted armament, but the type never advanced beyond flight trials. The US had further to go to catch up with the British and Germans who had backed jet research earlier.

The British provided General Electric with specifications for the Whittle engine, which was the basis for the Airacomet's propulsion. Early flight tests were relatively uneventful, but it was clear that thrust from the pair of General Electric I-A engines was deficient. Improved I-14 and I-16 engines, later designated J31-GE-5, boosted thrust to 2,000 pounds, but performance remained sluggish.

Three XP-59A test aircraft used British-built engines. These were followed by thirteen prototypes, designated YP-59A, which in turn were followed by twenty production P-59As. The final and most powerful variant was the P-59B, of which thirty entered service. Armament consisted of a cannon and three machine guns in the nose, but it was determined that the aircraft's handling and performance were not up to combat standards. A further fifty production units were cancelled and most of the remaining aircraft were assigned to Fourth Air Force's 412th Fighter Group where they were used as drones and airborne control platforms. In fact, odd as it may seem, some were modified with an open-cockpit in the nose to accommodate an observer for the drone missions.

As a fighter, the Airacomet was a disappointment and wisely it never went to war. Yet, it ushered the US into the jet era, providing valuable training for Army Air Forces personnel and establishing a practical foundation for development of later jet-powered aircraft like Lockheed's P-80 Shooting Star.

Specifications (for P-59B)
Manufacturer: Bell Aircraft
Type: single-seat jet fighter
Powerplant: two 2,000-lb thrust General Electric I-16 (J31-GE-5) centrifugal-flow turbojet engines
Wingspan: 45 ft 6 in
Length: 38 ft 2 in
Height: 12 ft 0 in
Maximum take-off weight: 13,700 lb
Maximum speed: 409 miles per hour
Cruising speed: 375 miles per hour
Service ceiling: 46,200 ft
Range: 400 miles
Armament: one nose-mounted 37-mm M4 cannon and three 0.5-in machine guns

Night Stalker: Northrop P-61 Black Widow

Radar came of age during World War II. Even before the success of the radar-based air defence system that ringed the British coastline, military strategists recognized the value of the sensor technology and sought to miniaturize it for use aboard aircraft. Britain made the essential breakthrough with development of the cavity magnetron. A high-powered vacuum tube generating microwaves, this device enabled the downsizing of radar sets so they could be installed in aircraft. A sample of the highly classified device was shared with US authorities in 1940, and later that year plans were begun for the world's first purpose-built, radar-equipped night fighter.

Perfecting the British AI (airborne interception) radar became the job of a joint British-American team working at the Radiation Laboratory of the Massachusetts Institute of Technology. The governmental priority for a combat-worthy airborne radar operable on centimetric wavelengths coupled with an exceptionally talented team of scientists from various disciplines led to successful airborne tests as early as the spring of 1941. The product that resulted was the Western Electric SCR-720 microwave airborne radar.

The Army Air Corps had contracted Northrop to design and produce the mission-specific aircraft. While the company under the leadership of its namesake, John K. 'Jack' Northrop, rightly held the reputation as one of the most creative and forward-leaning entities in the aviation industry, this project continued to be bogged down in an unremitting series of technical difficulties.

Designated P-61, the configuration entailed a twin-boom with a voluminous centre pod. The nose held the radar's scanning dish antenna and modulator. The lone pilot sat in a compartment just aft of the nose and immediately behind him was the radar operator/gunner in an elevated deck. A large portion of the pod accommodated the armament. Stacked on top in a remotely operated dorsal turret were four 0.5-in machine guns and below in a huge drooping belly fairing were four fixed forward-firing 20-mm cannon. The aft fuselage had a glazed tail cone for the radio operator/rear gunner.

The aircraft was gigantic for a fighter. It was more akin to an attack aircraft such as the Douglas A-20 Havoc. Interestingly enough, some Havocs were converted into radar-equipped night fighters and re-designated P-70s.

The P-61 was slow to go into production in part because the design had to integrate complex systems like an airborne radar. The type reached Britain in May 1944. Because of on-site training the first few P-61 squadrons had a delayed entry into combat. Nevertheless, this formation of P-61s is wearing D-Day invasion stripes.

Clearly, the P-61 wasn't going to dogfight like most fighters of the era, but rather premeditatedly stalk its prey at night through the marvel of cutting-edge electronics. Early models of the fighter were painted a glossy black to camouflage it in night's darkness. This caused the aircraft to be nicknamed the Black Widow.

The first flight occurred on 26 May 1942, but delays persisted. The YP-61 service test aircraft were finally fitted with the radar in April 1943. But once production of the P-61As began, a troubling quirk was discovered. When the automated dorsal turret rotated, violent tail buffeting was encountered. This led to an absence of the turret from some of the remaining models in that batch.

Once the gremlins were ironed out, the fighter handled responsively for an aircraft with so much mass. The two big Pratt & Whitney R-2800 radial engines ensured that the heavy fighter had adequate power. Black Widows were flown on their first operational night-fighting intercept mission in Europe on 3 July 1944. The type's first aerial victory was scored in the Pacific theatre three nights later.

The single biggest issue confronting the type once it began wartime operations was that enemy aircraft were relatively scarce through attrition from the grinding effects of the war's earlier years and the fact that the enemy was flying generally better-performing aircraft which made them harder to find within the night stalker's operating radius. Still, when Black Widow crews got a radar lock, the fighter's withering firepower was lethal.

Late in the war, some P-61s were used as intruders, taking out ground targets. After the war, others were converted to photo-reconnaissance platforms with the designation F-15A. The most numerous model was the P-61B of which 450 were built. Overall production was 706 units.

Specifications (for P-61B)
Manufacturer: Northrop
Type: three-seat night fighter
Powerplant: two 2,000-horsepower Pratt & Whitney R-2800-65 Double Wasp 18-cylinder radial engines
Wingspan: 66 ft ¾ in
Length: 49 ft 7 in
Height: 14 ft 8 in
Maximum take-off weight: 36,200 lb
Maximum speed: 366 miles per hour
Cruising speed: 229 miles per hour
Service ceiling: 33,100 ft
Range: 1,350 miles
Armament: four 20-mm M2 cannon, four 0.5-in machine guns, four 1,600-lb bombs

Big Brother: Bell P-63 King Cobra

Bell Aircraft began development of a latter model Airacobra, designated the XP-39E, which incorporated a laminar-flow wing and a taller vertical stabilizer/rudder. The company opted to start a whole new design based on this modified version of its existing fighter. The new aircraft was up-scaled and more powerful with the 1,325-horsepower Allison V-1710-93 engine.

The P-63 King Cobra was an improvement upon the P-39. When the newer type was ordered in June 1941, it represented an attempt to capitalize on the earlier aircraft's obvious strength, which was ground attack. The Soviets needed effective fighters in this role and they appreciated the destructive capacity of the type's 37-mm nose-mounted cannon, two 0.5-in nose-mounted machine guns and two 0.5-in wing-mounted machine guns.

Of the 3,362 P-63s produced, 2,456 were exported to the Soviet Union under the Lend Lease program. Another 300 were provided to Free French forces. The US did not use any in combat. Most of the production run comprised the P-63A and the P-63C. The latter used the 1,800-horsepower Allison V-1716-117 engine with water injection to boost power even more in spurts. The King Cobra's cannon, like the P-39's, could pierce virtually any mobile armour, so it gained a reputation as a prolific tank buster.

In the final year of the war, 300 A and C models were transformed into manned targets, as strange as that sounds. The aircraft, designated RP-63A and RP-63C, were sheathed in a cocoon of duralumin alloy. Also, the modification involved the use of hollowed-out propellers and bulletproof glass. Thankfully, aerial gunnery trainees used only frangible bullets which disintegrated harmlessly upon contact, though one must wonder what the pilots of the target aircraft felt like during those target practice missions. The target aircraft were rigged to flash

Basically, an improved version of the P-39, the P-63 King Cobra was an effective tank buster because of its 37-mm cannon.

red lights when the students scored, and in appropriate jest these models were referred to as Pinballs.

With the King Cobra, Bell Aircraft perpetuated the baseline configuration of its earlier P-39, which placed the engine behind the cockpit and gave primacy to the large cannon whose barrel protruded through the aircraft's spinner. For the Soviets, the aircraft served the purpose of helping to repulse the armour of German ground forces. The P-63 had limited application, but it performed that proscribed function with satisfactory results.

Specifications (for P-63A)
Manufacturer: Bell Aircraft
Type: single-seat fighter
Powerplant: one 1,325-horsepower Allison V-1710-93 liquid-cooled V-12 engine
Wingspan: 38 ft 4 in
Length: 32 ft 8 in
Height: 12 ft 7 in
Maximum take-off weight: 10,500 lb
Maximum speed: 410 miles per hour
Cruising speed: 378 miles per hour
Service ceiling: 43,000 ft
Range: 450 miles
Armament: one nose-mounted 37-mm cannon and two nose-mounted 0.5-in machine guns, two 0.5-in machine guns in underwing pods, up to three 500-lb bombs

Fighting Kitten: Grumman F4F Wildcat

Through the mid-1930s, the US Navy was enamoured of biplane fighters. But change was in the offing as design theory was increasingly shifting to monoplanes as the preferred configuration, especially where speed was a paramount consideration. In 1936, the little-known Brewster company won the service's new fighter competition with its entry of a squat monoplane. Called the Buffalo, this aircraft became the US Navy's first operational monoplane fighter.

Alarmed by the setback, Grumman, which had offered a biplane design, worked feverishly to prepare a monoplane design for submittal. The US Navy was interested and Grumman flew its new XF4F-2 prospect for the first time on 2 September 1937. In comparison with the Buffalo, the Grumman entry was minimally faster but considerably less manoeuvrable. Not discouraged, Grumman revised its design and most importantly upgraded the engine to the Pratt & Whitney Twin Wasp XR-1830-76 with a two-stage supercharger.

Grumman's improvements brought substantially higher speed. Further refinements to the aircraft's fin resulted in better handling. With the progress in performance, the US Navy recognized that Grumman's design was superior and began to order F4F-3 models in August 1939. The French *Aéronavale* had ordered a quantity as well, but by the time the aircraft were ready for delivery in the summer of 1940, France had fallen. Those aircraft were diverted to Britain where they were nicknamed Martlets. The following year, a Martlet in Fleet Air Arm service scored a kill against a German intruder, becoming the first air-to-air victory for the type.

When Grumman's monoplane fighter attained operational readiness with a couple of US Navy fighter squadrons, the Wildcat nickname was adopted. This represented the beginning of the 'cat' identity for a long and distinguished line of naval fighters built by Grumman.

The Wildcat was a pudgy mid-wing design that reflected the transition from biplane to monoplane in that the monoplane's fuselage bore the general rotund appearance of the company's preceding design, the F3F biplane fighter. The monoplane was more streamlined and it had a large area wing with squared tips. The quintessential model was the F4F-4, which began to reach front-line Navy and Marine squadrons, a month before the Japanese attack on Pearl Harbor on 7 December 1941.

The Wildcat soon began to etch a place for itself in the pantheon of great fighters. Only a few days after Pearl Harbor, Marines flying the fighter in the ultimately doomed defence of Wake Island fought valiantly against overwhelming numbers. The Marines again showed their mettle and proved the value of the Wildcat in August 1942 when they participated in air operations out of Guadalcanal's Henderson Field.

Memorably, on 20 February 1942, while at the controls of his Wildcat, Edward 'Butch' O'Hare of VF-42 almost single-handedly saved his aircraft carrier, the USS *Lexington*, in waters near Rabaul. He shot down five enemy attack aircraft that it is likely would have sunk or disabled the ship otherwise. The Naval Academy graduate who was raised in Chicago became the US Navy's first ace of the war and was awarded the Medal of Honor. Much later, Chicago's main airport was named in his memory.

A few months later, at Coral Sea and then at Midway, Wildcats flying off the USS *Enterprise*, USS *Saratoga*, and USS *Hornet* performed brilliantly. The former battle was the first in history where the fighting occurred between naval vessels that were not in sight of one another. The outcome was inconclusive but a sign that America could at least hold its own against the

Two famous naval pilots are seen in formation flying Grumman F4F Wildcats. In the lead is Jimmy Thach, known for developing the 'Thach Weave' fighter tactic, and the wingman is Butch O'Hare, the US Navy's first ace of World War II who was honoured posthumously with the naming of Chicago's main airport in his memory.

Japanese fleet. At Midway, the first major US naval victory was secured and signalled the turning of fortunes in the Pacific theatre.

The Wildcat was arguably a notch inferior to its nemesis, the Mitsubishi Zero, but with excellent training, improvised tactics and perhaps most of all the grit and skill of the pilots, incredible odds were surmounted. Legendary naval aviator Jimmy Thach devised the 'Thach Weave' to counter the Wildcat's inherent disadvantage when encountering Japanese fighters. In general, like the Flying Tigers in P-40s, the Wildcat pilots sought to score in the first pass and not become enmeshed in a protracted melee.

The Wildcat held the line in the Pacific until more advanced naval fighters could reach the front by the middle of the war. Even after the newer fighters started to arrive in 1943, the Wildcat continued to be employed, mainly aboard the many escort carriers.

Total production of the Wildcat was 7,885. Of these, an amazing 5,237 were built under licence by the Eastern Division of General Motors. The aircraft produced by the Eastern Division were designated the FM-1 and the FM-2, the difference between these two models

A development of the 1930s, the Wildcat was at a comparable disadvantage to the latest Japanese fighters it encountered, but with excellent and highly motivated pilots at the controls it managed to score against the enemy and provide the breathing space necessary before the next generation of fighters could reach the fleet.

being that the latter was powered by the 1,350-horsepower Wright R-1820-56 Cyclone 9 radial engine.

Specifications (for F4F-4)
Manufacturer: Grumman
Type: single-seat carrier-borne fighter
Powerplant: one 1,200-horsepower Pratt & Whitney R-1830-36 Twin Wasp 14-cylinder radial piston engine
Wingspan: 38 ft 0 in
Length: 28 ft 9 in
Height: 9 ft 2 in
Maximum take-off weight: 7,952 lb
Maximum speed: 318 miles per hour
Cruising speed: 155 miles per hour
Service ceiling: 39,400 ft
Range: 770 miles
Armament: six 0.5-in Browning machine guns, two 100-lb bombs

Ferocious Feline: Grumman F6F Hellcat

In the late summer of 1943, the Grumman F6F Hellcat joined the fight in the Pacific, and any lingering doubt about the war's eventual outcome was soon allayed because the new and powerful fighter, generated in vast numbers from America's dynamic aviation industry, represented the evolution in front-line aircraft needed to match and to exceed the enemy's flying arsenal. Development of the type had begun even before the Japanese attack on Pearl Harbor and the lessons learned from the earlier Wildcat, corporately, aeronautically and militarily, were applied to the new aircraft.

The Hellcat was beefier and more capable in every respect than its predecessor. The brutish Pratt & Whitney Double Wasp, with its two-row cylinder arrangement, ensured higher speeds and faster climb rates. The fuselage went from the Wildcat's conveniently circular shape to a robust pear shape. An increase in wing area enhanced range and low-speed handling qualities which are critical for carrier operations.

Another big improvement was the landing gear placement. With the Wildcat, the gear folded up into the bottom of the forward fuselage; whereas, the main gear on the Hellcat

Grumman's follow-on fighter to the Wildcat was the exceptional Hellcat. The type performed admirably in the Pacific theatre, destroying more enemy aircraft than any other US Navy carrier-borne aircraft. Starting in mid-1943, some Hellcats were made expressly for the night fighter mission and these featured a pod on the starboard wing for the APS-6 radar.

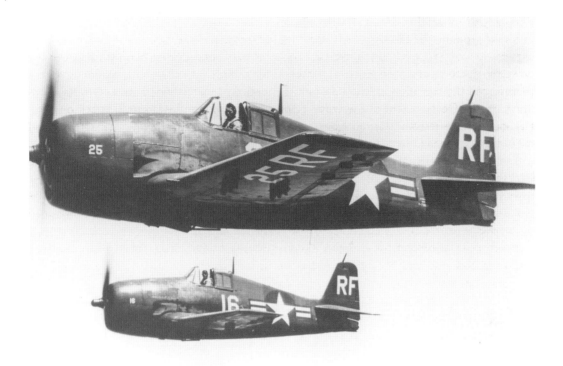

Grumman became known for its naval fighters of World War II and beyond, each of which was identified as some sort of 'cat.' When referring to this lineage, people often speak of the Grumman cats. From the archetypal Wildcat all the way to the jet-age Tomcat, these Grumman aircraft were acclaimed for their durability. These F6F Hellcats are in the markings of the naval reserve.

retracted into wells in the wings. This allowed for a most welcomed wider stance and thereby lessened ground-looping tendencies.

Because Grumman's engineering staff paid attention to reports from the field regarding their earlier fighter, they crafted a new fighter that was tailor-made for the Pacific air war. By listening to those who had accumulated experience in the crucible of combat, the company succeeded in conceiving a superb all-around fighter to decisively take control of the air. The Hellcat's design success is reflected by the fact that the fighter, once deployed, required almost no further updating other than add-on systems.

The two major production versions were the F6F-3 and the F6F-5 of which 4,402 and 6,341 were built, respectively. The differences between the two models were relatively minor. The latter had a more powerful version of the Pratt & Whitney R-2800 that incorporated water injection. While Grumman farmed out most of its production on the Wildcat to General Motors, the Hellcat was churned out at its Bethpage, Long Island, New York, facilities with the production run totalling 12,274.

To counter Japanese night operations, some Hellcats were pressed into the night interception role. Hunter-killer teams were formed in which a TBF Avenger, outfitted with bulky airborne radar, would comb the night skies in unison with several Hellcats. If enemy aircraft were detected, the Hellcats would be vectored to them. Sadly, not quite two years after saving USS *Lexington*, 'Butch' O'Hare was shot down in one of these missions. Adding to the tragedy is that subsequent evidence suggests the shoot-down may have occurred due to a friendly fire mix-up. Eventually, certain Hellcats were equipped for the night fighter role with the APS-6 radar, in which the antenna was carried in a dedicated wing pod.

Among the best-known Hellcat pilots was David McCampbell. During his rise to command the air group aboard the USS *Essex*, he led from the front and accumulated an ever growing tally of air-to-air victories. Notably, at the Battle of the Philippine Seas and the Battle of Leyte Gulf he scored multiple kills. By war's end his total count was thirty-four, the highest of any naval aviator. Captain McCampbell was awarded the Medal of Honor.

The Hellcat's contribution to securing Pacific skies is clear from the statistics regarding the Pacific theatre's air fighting. Of the 6,477 enemy aircraft destroyed by the US Navy's carrier-borne pilots, 4,947 fell victim to the guns of Hellcats. Because of its inherent strengths and substantial numbers, the Hellcat did more to wrest mastery of the air from the once seemingly invincible Japanese than any other naval fighter.

Specifications (for F6F-5)
Manufacturer: Grumman
Type: single-seat carrier-borne fighter/bomber
Powerplant: one 2,000-horsepower Pratt & Whitney R-2800-10W Double Wasp 18-cylinder radial piston engine
Wingspan: 42 ft 10 in (16 ft 2 in wings folded)
Length: 33 ft 7 in
Height: 13 ft 1 in
Maximum take-off weight: 15,413 lb
Maximum speed: 386 miles per hour
Cruising speed: 168 miles per hour
Service ceiling: 37,300 ft
Range: 1,040 miles (internal fuel)
Armament: six 0.5-in Browning machine guns, up to 2,000 lb in bombs or six rockets

Bent-wing Bird: Vought F4U Corsair

Seeking to improve upon its first monoplane fighters, the US Navy sought proposals for a second wave of more advanced fighters. In mid-1938, the company that would evolve as Chance Vought Aircraft received a contract for a promising design that would incorporate the massive two-row radial engine of sister company, Pratt & Whitney, which, like Vought, was controlled at the time by conglomerate United Aircraft. However, unlike Grumman's development of the Hellcat, which was predicated on an earlier design and which moved ahead briskly, Vought's clean-sheet Corsair proved to be a slow, laborious fighter development in its carrier-borne version. Thankfully, the resulting aircraft was worth the wait.

The prototype XF4U-1 first flew on 29 May 1940. Conspicuously, the wings had an inverted-gull shape, as if a 'V' were sculpted into the wing outboard of the root. This oddity was adopted, in part, to provide the particularly large-diameter Hamilton-Standard propeller

Many F4U Corsairs were shore-based and this scene depicts a typical squadron start-up and taxi out. Note the ground crewman directing the end aircraft as dust and sand are kicked up by the prop wash.

Looking worn but still very formidable, these Corsairs have been finessed into precise formation. The fighter's unique 'bent-wing' endures as the type's defining feature.

blades with adequate ground clearance. By connecting the two main landing gear legs at the wings' low point, it was possible to shorten the gear and thus to fully retract it in the wings. The distinctive form caused many observers to invoke the term 'bent-wing' when referring to the aircraft.

Not long after its flight test programme began, the prototype was badly damaged in a forced landing and its repair set the programme back several months. When the Corsair flew again in the autumn, it exceeded 400 miles per hour in level flight. This was a first for any US military aircraft and spoke volumes about both the fighter's sleek design and powerful engine. Indeed, at that point Pratt & Whitney chose to focus its attention on its traditional air-cooled radial engines rather than develop potentially more problematical liquid-cooled engines.

The initial excitement was dampened by a series of design changes that called for relocating all machine guns in the wings and placing all fuel in a fuselage tank. This necessitated moving the cockpit aft by nearly three feet, which, in turn, reduced pilot visibility. Production models began arriving in July 1942, but it was discovered that they were laden with handling characteristics that precluded their use on aircraft carriers.

Landing on aircraft carriers is a tricky business under even ideal conditions and the Corsair at this point in its progression exhibited an alarming disparity in stall onset between its wings. There was also a sideways motion when flaring just before touching down. Under the circumstances, the Corsair was assigned to land-based squadrons, the first being VMF-124, a Marine outfit in the Pacific. Perhaps the most famous Marine squadron to fly the Corsair was VMF-214, known as the 'Black Sheep' and commanded by the cantankerous ace Gregory 'Pappy' Boyington.

Because of the high-pitched sound the Corsair made when swooping down in fast low-level runs, the Japanese referred to the fighter as 'Whistling Death.' The type was viewed on both sides as the most awesome fighter in the theatre of operations. In the end, the Corsair's kill/loss ratio in Navy and Marine service was an impressive eleven to one.

The limitations on the Corsair were addressed so that, eventually, US Navy carrier operations for the type were approved. Interestingly, the British Fleet Air Arm was first to use the Corsair as a carrier-borne fighter. Among notable engagements in Royal Navy service, the Corsair participated in operations against the German warship *Tirpitz*.

Special accommodations for the Corsair had to be made on British carriers. The height of the hangar bays was inadequate when the Corsair's wings were folded upright during storage below decks. Eight inches had to be lopped off each Corsair wing.

To meet the demand for the well-regarded Navy and Marine fighter, Goodyear and Brewster began producing the FG-1 and F3A models, respectively. The last wartime production model was the F4U-4. This aircraft featured various improvements including a better cockpit and the 2,450-horsepower version of the Pratt & Whitney R-2800 engine.

As a tribute to its outstanding performance, the Corsair was the last piston-powered fighter to be built in the US, production not ceasing until 1952. It was used effectively in ground attack missions during the Korean War, operating from carriers alongside newly introduced jets. Also, it remained in French naval service up to October 1964. The final production count was 12,571.

Specifications (for F4U-1)
Manufacturer: Vought Aircraft
Type: single-seat carrier-borne fighter/bomber
Powerplant: one 2,000-horsepower Pratt & Whitney R-2800-8 Double Wasp 18-cylinder radial piston engine
Wingspan: 41 ft 0 in
Length: 33 ft 4 in
Height: 16 ft 1 in
Maximum take-off weight: 14,000 lb
Maximum speed: 417 miles per hour
Cruising speed: 182 miles per hour
Service ceiling: 36,900 ft
Range: 1,015 miles
Armament: six 0.5-in Browning machine guns (later variants equipped with four 20-mm cannon, two 1,000-lb bombs)

Steadfast Defender: Hawker Hurricane

In the mid-1930s, the air forces of the industrial powers began the transition from biplanes to monoplanes. Britain did so with its renowned Hurricane fighter. The Hurricane sprang from the technical expertise, trendsetting handiwork and lissom imagination of design visionary Sydney Camm. A Hawker engineer with a line of well-regarded biplanes to his credit, Camm only partly broke the mould with his new aircraft.

Instead of all-metal construction, the Hurricane had a tubular steel airframe with aluminium stringers and ribs covered by fabric. It was configured around the new Rolls-Royce V-12 liquid-cooled engine. Unlike its biplane predecessors, the Hurricane had retractable landing gear. Moreover, instead of nose-mounted or rear ring-mounted machine guns, the Hurricane's thick camber wings accommodated eight 0.303-in machine guns.

First flight occurred on 6 November 1935. With a top speed in excess of 300 miles per hour, the Hurricane was an encouraging start to the paradigmatic change in fighter architecture. Orders were placed and by 1937 the type entered service with RAF squadrons. By August 1940, as the Battle of Britain commenced, thirty-two RAF squadrons were flying the Hurricane.

The Hurricane was not quite up to par with the faster Messerschmitt Bf 109. A significant handicap was the two-bladed fixed-pitch wooden propeller on the Hurricane Mk I, but the type was highly manoeuvrable, rugged, well armed, and easily serviced and maintained. To the extent possible, the less numerous but more effective Spitfire would engage the enemy fighters while the Hurricane was the preferred interceptor against the *Luftwaffe* bombers.

Despite their shortcomings, Hurricanes shot down more than half the encroaching German aircraft during 1940. Unquestionably, Hurricanes were the RAF's workhorses of the Battle of Britain. Their contribution to winning that pivotal summer-long air battle can hardly be overstated.

The Mk II appeared in September 1940. This model was built in the greatest number. Power was bumped up with the installation of the 1,280-horsepower Rolls-Royce Merlin XX. Depending on the sub-variant, the wing was modified to house twelve machine guns or four

20-mm cannon. A capability to carry two 500-lb bombs was also added. A further sub-variant was armed with two under-wing 40-mm antitank cannon. This firepower proved devastating in the North Africa campaign.

The Hurricane was adapted for aircraft carrier operations as the Sea Hurricane, but first was deployed on catapult-equipped merchantmen. Beginning in 1941, Sea Hurricanes provided convoy protection in the Atlantic, succeeding in downing several Focke-Wulf Fw 200 Condors. Later, in a three-day defence of a Malta-bound convoy, Sea Hurricanes operating from three Royal Navy ships shot down thirty-nine enemy aircraft while losing only eight of their own. Interestingly, the Sea Hurricane was never modified with folding wings.

The third and final major model was the Mk IV which was notable for its so-called 'universal wing.' This wing allowed for the fitting of the full inventory of fighter-sized bombs, rockets, guns, and drop tanks. The Mk IV, which emerged in March 1943, had the 1,620-horsepower Merlin 24 engine optimized for low-altitude flight as increasingly the type was being used in the fighter-bomber role.

The RAF sent fighter squadrons to France as German forces advanced through Europe, ever closer to Britain. It was hoped that the Third Reich could be blunted before it reached across the English Channel. In this scene, RAF pilots of No. 87 Squadron practise a scramble to their Hurricane Mk I fighters at an airfield in the French countryside in December 1939. Despite a valiant effort, the Battle of France was lost a short time later. As a result, this scene was repeated many times in England during the summer and autumn of 1940. With Hurricanes in the lead, the Battle of Britain turned the tide against the intruders and prevented a full-scale invasion.

In assessing the Hurricane, its versatility stands out. Its many applications included night fighter and photo-reconnaissance platform. Chances are that the Hurricane will be remembered as the fighter that came in the nick of time to repel German attackers and rescue Britain from catastrophe. Though the Hurricane's performance was less than stellar by the time the conflict spread to the homeland's skies, Sydney Camm's immortal creation was up to the job.

Production concluded in 1944 when the Hurricane, with its roots stretching well back into the 1930s, ran out of further upgrades. Newer aircraft had surpassed it, but the reliable fighter remained in RAF service until 1947. Production totalled 14,233 with Hawker's output supplemented by Gloster, Canadian Car and Foundry, and Fairey.

Specifications (for Mk I)
Manufacturer: Hawker
Type: single-seat interceptor/fighter
Powerplant: one 1,030-horsepower Rolls-Royce Merlin III liquid-cooled V-12 engine
Wingspan: 40 ft 0 in
Length: 31 ft 4 in
Height: 13 ft 4½ in
Maximum take-off weight: 6,218 lb
Maximum speed: 308 miles per hour
Cruising speed: 212 miles per hour
Service ceiling: 33,400 ft
Range: 525 miles
Armament: eight 0.303-in Browning machine guns

Elliptical Beauty: Supermarine Spitfire
No other World War II aircraft has quite captured the public imagination like the illustrious Spitfire. Conceived in the fertile mind of design genius Reginald J. Mitchell, the Spitfire drew on the successful designs that Mitchell had created for the Schneider Cup Races. Mitchell strove to achieve a purity of form and function, a simple elegance. As many have said, the curvaceous fighter that first soared above the English countryside around Southampton on 5 March 1936 was the ultimate combination of grace with purpose in a military aircraft.

Most importantly, the Supermarine S.6B floatplane, which won the coveted Scheider trophy in 1931 with a blazing speed of nearly 340 miles per hour, was powered by the new Rolls-Royce R, an engine that had evolved from the company's Buzzard design, which itself came from the V-12 Kestrel of the 1920s. These pioneering liquid-cooled engines represented the foundation of what became the acclaimed Merlin engine, an exquisite machine expertly crafted by hand, that provided reliable power at levels enabling superlative performance in the unforgiving arena of air combat.

When the Merlin was mated with the Spitfire, it was the perfect marriage of brawn with beauty, potency with potential, vim with vision. The 990-horsepower engine in the first Spitfire prototype would be eclipsed soon and again with succeeding versions of the Merlin throughout the war. The prototype's attained speed of 350 miles per hour was a portent of the greatness to come.

The Battle of Britain raged through the summer and autumn of 1940, and the homeland defence depended in large part on the highly manoeuvrable Spitfire. In this photograph of 24 July 1940, the two closest aircraft are Spitfire Mk IAs of the RAF's No. 610 Squadron which operated out of Biggen Hill in Kent.

The classic elliptical wing is evident in this view of a Spitfire Mk VB of the RAF's No. 92 Squadron on 19 May 1941. Although this aircraft was shot down by a Messerschmitt Bf 109 a month later, the growing numbers of Spitfires reaching front-line squadrons steadily began to turn the tables on the *Luftwaffe*.

The Spitfire was an all-metal aircraft, small in overall dimension but sporting a wide-chord elliptical wing that accommodated four 0.303-in machine guns on each side. The streamlined configuration minimized drag and emphasized agility, the prized attribute craved by fighter pilots. The monoplane with retractable landing gear was a definitive break from Britain's long history of biplane fighters. Its bold yet aesthetic silhouette signalled the vanguard of a new generation of military aircraft.

By the time the looming storm struck over the homeland in the summer of 1940, there were nineteen RAF squadrons equipped with the Spitfire. RAF Fighter Command valiantly thwarted the intruding *Luftwaffe* fighters and bombers thanks, in part, to the Spitfires that had been produced and deployed. The ensuing clash was possibly the most consequential aerial conflict in history. The Battle of Britain pitted the best of the two adversaries against one another in a do-or-die fight to the finish.

With so much riding in the balance, it was fortuitous that the Spitfire compared favourably with the Messerschmitt Bf 109. In addition, the RAF had the benefit of the Home Chain system of coastal radar sites, which were linked to filter stations and central command centres. Through an integrated network, the defenders were vectored to the approaching swarms. Around London, ordinary citizens could observe the air war unfold before their eyes as the two leading fighter types from both sides duelled for control of the sky.

Before the end of that year, the second production model, the Spitfire Mk II, rolled out of the factory in two main sub-variants, each of which had a more powerful Merlin than the original production model, the Mk I. This kind of upgrade was to occur with regularity throughout the war. Indeed, by war's end the Spitfire had been advanced technologically to the point where, in its last major model, its speed had risen by 100 miles per hour from the peak level of the maiden model.

In March 1941, the Spitfire Mk V started to arrive. Some had clipped wings and armament varied. The standard complement was eight machine guns while others had a combination of four machine guns and two cannon or four cannon only. Horsepower was bumped up in keeping with the wartime pattern. More than 7,000 of this model were built.

Some of the Mk Vs were dispatched to other theatres such as Malta, the Middle East, and the Pacific. This model also carried the air war back over the continent. While operating over France in September 1941, the Focke-Wulf Fw 190 was encountered for the first time and it became apparent instantly that the new *Luftwaffe* fighter outclassed the Mk V. By July 1942, the Spitfire Mk IX arrived on the scene and, with its improved Merlin engine, it restored the balance between opposing fighter types.

The next big leap came with the introduction of the Mk XII in 1943. This model was powered by the Rolls-Royce Griffon engine, a derivative of the famed Merlin. An immediate improvement in low-altitude speed was achieved.

Later, a two-stage, two-speed supercharger was added to the Griffon and this engine was installed in the Mk XIV. These were the best all-around air combat versions from the programme's beginning through to 1944. In addition to excelling in air-to-air engagements, they intercepted V-1 buzz bombs and flew ground attack missions.

A navalized Spitfire was seen as a partial answer to the woefully outdated carrier-borne aircraft of the Royal Navy at the outset of the war. Spitfire Mk VBs were converted into Seafires through airframe strengthening and the addition of arrester hooks. As Seafire Mk IBs, these fighters entered service in June 1942. Late in the year, they participated in North African operations aboard HMS *Furious*. The most numerous model was the Seafire Mk III which had manually folding wings.

A stunning 20,351 Spitfires in all forms were produced before, during and after the war, an intrinsic tribute to the validity of the underlying design. In the hands of memorable pilots like the American Eagle Squadron volunteers, the indefatigable legless ace Douglas Bader, the highest scoring Commonwealth ace Johnnie Johnson, and many more, the Spitfire symbolized the rise and eventual triumph of the human spirit against the sinister and cascading forces of despotism.

Specifications (for Mk V)
Manufacturer: Supermarine
Type: single-seat fighter
Powerplant: one 1,470 horsepower Rolls-Royce Merlin 45M/50M/55M liquid-cooled V-12 engine
Wingspan: 32 ft 2 in
Length: 29 ft 11 in
Height: 9 ft 11 in
Maximum take-off weight: 6,650 lb
Maximum speed: 357 miles per hour
Cruising speed: 272 miles per hour
Service ceiling: 35,500 ft
Range: 470 miles
Armament: two 20-mm Hispano cannon, four 0.303-in Browning machine guns, up to 500 lb in bombs with modification

Chapter 4

Striking from the Sky:
Mud Runners and Heavies

During World War II, persistence was the hallmark of the long-range heavy bomber crews. Some missions lasted more than half a day. Navigating to the target was rarely easy, especially given the comparatively primitive on-board instrumentation coupled with the prevailing weather patterns over continental Europe and East Anglia in England – the launch/recovery point for most aircraft of the famed Eighth Air Force.

On many missions, the bombers encountered flak-filled skies once they reached their targets. Both before their bomb runs and following bombs away, they were subject to swarms of enemy interceptors plunging into their neat, well-rehearsed formations. According to pre-war air power theory, as it developed at the Air Tactical School at Langley Field and later at Maxwell Field, the modern bomber was a veritable fortress in the sky, a nearly invincible weapon that was destined to enjoy primacy.

But, as the crews of the US Army Air Forces soon learned once their strategic bombers started operating out of bases in England in 1942, the theorists' concepts proved invalid in the real-world of hostile skies. The modern bomber, festooned with numerous defensive gun positions, was supposed to be virtually indestructible. The presumption was that the new hulking aircraft would be able to fend off any attackers. When clustered together in tight formations, each bomber would form a chink in an impenetrable and heavily armed moving wall.

The reality was that the Messerschmitts and Focke-Wulfs got through the concentrated and overlapping cones of fire that looked so impressive on paper. The sheer closing speed of fast-cruising bombers and power-diving interceptors made identifying, tracking, and shooting enemy fighters a more gruelling challenge than had been imagined. Indeed, the *Luftwaffe* quickly determined the vulnerabilities of the new bombers and exploited them with ruthless efficiency. The first B-17s deployed to the theatre were lightly armed in the nose and not surprisingly German interceptors made head-on passes, guns blazing, with little return fire from the beleaguered Flying Forts.

Boeing corrected the defensive weakness with the introduction of the G model, which had a forward-firing chin turret. Despite these kinds of design improvements, the situation remained dire, with attrition rates reaching alarming levels. The Americans could hardly sustain the ongoing losses. Damage was inflicted on some of the German war-making apparatus, but at too terrible a price. Something had to give.

The answer came with the introduction of the long-range escort fighter. The P-51 was not only able to accompany bombers on lengthy missions, but when enemy fighters were encountered the Mustang was more than a match. The playing field was levelled and, at last, the bombers could deliver the devastating blow that had been envisioned by the pre-war air power advocates.

While the Americans doggedly pursued daylight precision bombing centred around the then top-secret Norden bombsight, the British opted for ostensibly safer night bombing. As the air war ensued, the weaponry and tactics evolved rapidly into an ever shifting cat-and-mouse game in which night fighters, equipped with the latest variant of airborne radar, would catch Lancasters unawares, shooting bursts that caused sudden fiery balls of fire that brilliantly illuminated the night sky. Countermeasures like chaff were employed to thwart the opposing technology, and the tides kept alternating until near war's end when the weight of the massed Allied raids became too much.

Despite the genius of the Norden bombsight, it proved impractical in that there were just too many variables on a typical mission. Factors such as winds, clouds and airspeeds played havoc with the bombardier's aiming. On certain missions, it was difficult just to make positive identification of the target.

Sometimes it took several bomb groups flying in waves and unloading massive tonnage to place a handful of bombs on the designated target. Though it isn't fair to compare attempts at exactitude in targeting during World War II to today's precision air strikes, by their huge volume of delivered ordnance the bombers of the 1940s had discernible effect. What was missing in accuracy was compensated for by sheer mass.

After nearly three years of progressively more punishing aerial attacks, German petroleum stocks were whittled to subsistence levels and no matter how hard *Luftwaffe* commanders tried, there wasn't sufficient fuel to mount an effective air defence. The Allies had gained control of the 'high ground', which meant that the Third *Reich* wouldn't last much longer. Even the appearance of Germany's vaunted wonder weapons like the V-2 rocket and the Me 262 *Schwalbe* were not enough to stem the tide of defeat.

In the Pacific theatre, a futuristic shape cast its imposing shadow over Japan. The massive B-29 Superfortress was unlike any other bomber developed up to that time. In almost every way, it outperformed its predecessors. With cigar-chomping Curtis LeMay in charge, the bombers pummelled the mainland with napalm and then with two atomic weapons in attacks that remain controversial generations later. The war ended soon after, however, and the dreaded amphibious assault on the Japanese home islands, which many expected to be far bloodier than the brutal preparatory island-hopping campaign, was averted.

Night Pounder: Avro Lancaster

Judging from its inauspicious beginnings, the Lancaster hardly seemed like the aircraft that would end up as Britain's foremost wartime heavy bomber. It evolved from the Avro Manchester, a twin-engine bomber conceived in the pre-war period in parallel with two other British heavy bombers, the Handley Page Halifax and the Short Stirling. While expectations were high for all three, only the Halifax rendered respectable performance.

The Manchester's problem pertained to its Rolls-Royce Vulture engines. They were extraordinarily complex and failed to provide adequate power at the higher altitudes. Rather than scrap the whole project, Rolls-Royce and Avro designer Roy Chadwick devised a solution

Photographing warbirds, like this North American Aviation P-51D, in their natural element was William Slate's passion.

The Vultee BT-13 Valiant was known as the Vibrator because when aerodynamically stalled a pronounced elevator buffet occurs which notably shakes the empennage, wings and canopy. This restoration of the intermediate trainer is on static display during an air show. It is adorned in the classic Army training colours of blue fuselage, yellow wings and candy-stripe rudder.

The BT-13A in the foreground is joined in formation by a North American Aviation BT-14, known in Canada as a Yale Mk I. This photograph provides an opportunity to compare the two basic trainers. Both aircraft used the 450-horsepower Pratt & Whitney R-985 engine, but the BT-14 is easily distinguishable because of its wheel strut fairings. Only a few hundred BT-14s were built.

An AT-6D rises from the runway's sea of concrete and the landing gear can be seen retracting into the wings. In the 1980s, it was common to see the type in Spanish Air Force markings because used trainers from Spain were being imported to the US at the time. Eventually, most of these were repainted in standard wartime US training colours.

The Airacobra was flown by a number of foreign air forces. In the summer of 1941, the RAF received a variant based on the P-39D, but decided to withdraw the type because of disappointing speed and deficient high-altitude performance, among other reasons. The Soviet Union was the largest user, successfully employing mainly the P-39Q as a tank buster. Late in the war, Free French units also operated mostly the Q model.

America's most ubiquitous post-war Lightning was Marvin 'Lefty' Gardner's bright white P-38 nicknamed *White Lit'nin*. A fixture for many years at the annual Reno air races, the aircraft was a favourite among the fans. Gardner had been a bomber pilot in World War II who yearned to fly fighters. After the war, he set up a crop dusting service in Texas and bought the Lightning for fun which empowered him to fly his fighter of choice to his heart's content. An accident followed by prohibitive repair costs precluded his continued ownership. The aircraft was transferred to Europe where it got a complete makeover. (*Photo by Philip Handleman*)

A two-ship formation of brightly restored Texans shows the kind of training US Army and Navy cadets received during World War II.

Like most World War II fighters, there are few flyable Republic P-47 Thunderbolts left so when one does appear on the air show scene, it is a special treat. This restored P-47 graced the ramp amid warbirds at the Madera, California, air show in 1985 shortly after an extensive rebuild at Chino, California.

Despite the fact that P-40s were built in enormous quantities, only a few remain airworthy. Occasionally, one can be observed at fly-ins and air shows.

One of the most famous forms of nose art was the shark's teeth of the American Volunteer Group, popularly known as the Flying Tigers. Under the leadership of Claire Chennault, this group overcame tremendous odds to rack up impressive aerial victories. The tactics developed helped to compensate for the antiquated fighter. The pictured aircraft sports the Flying Tigers emblem on the fuselage. The P-40 was on display at the Tico Air Show in Florida.

One of the best known P-51D restorations is *Crazy Horse* which is often seen at air shows with the masterful Lee Lauderback at the controls. Lauderback is in the forefront of warbird restorers/operators who strive to keep the old warplanes airworthy. At a flight school in Florida, Lauderback and colleagues help other warbird pilots to maintain proficiency. Flying skills are as important as well-maintained equipment.

Today's warbird pilots may not know what it was like to gyrate through life-and-death dogfights in the hostile skies of Europe or the Pacific during World War II, but they do have the opportunity to feel at least some of the sensations experienced by the original pilots who occupied the cockpits of the wartime fighters. In a scene reminiscent of an escort fighter returning to base after a long day's mission, a P-51D nicknamed *Jumpin' Jacques*, pierces a pink and blue horizon, soon to reach its destination for the night.

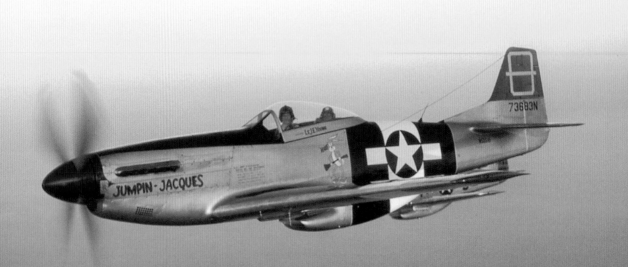

A role for night fighters had developed even before America entered World War II. In the US, Northrop developed the P-61 Black Widow, which was the country's first aircraft designed and built expressly to be a night fighter. The four-barrelled dorsal turret could be devastating if locked onto a target at close enough range. This is a P-61A in flight over metropolitan Los Angeles. The next production model had a fitting all-black paint scheme.

Sydney Camm, Hawker's brilliant designer, conceived the Hurricane well in advance of the pivotal Battle of Britain. Rugged and well armed, the fighter provided valuable service in defense of the homeland.

The Corsair was originated by Vought, but later on Goodyear built the aircraft with a more powerful 2,250-horsepower water-injected engine under the designation FG-1. These did not have folding wings since they were intended solely for shore-based operations. Some of these models became popular for air racing in the post-war years.

A closer view of the F4U-1 showcases the meticulous restoration. It is an accepted irony among warbird enthusiasts that many restored warplanes are in better condition with glossier paint, more dependable parts, preferred avionics, etc. than when the originals first rolled off the assembly lines in the 1940s.

Among the rarest of warbirds is the elegant Spitfire. More than sixty-five years after World War II ended, only a precious few of the legendary fighters are now flying. This Spitfire Mk IX is a two-seat trainer conversion.

The four-engine Avro Lancaster was Britain's premier heavy bomber. It was a mainstay of the night bombing raids against Germany.

Only about fifteen Boeing B-17 Flying Fortresses remain airworthy worldwide. Maintenance costs are prohibitive and it is only volunteer efforts of non-profit organizations that keep the big aircraft flying. The Collings Foundation of Stow, Massachusetts, has operated the B-17G *Nine-O-Nine* for many years. Produced too late for combat, this aircraft is decorated in the markings of a bomber with the 323rd Bomb Squadron, 91st Bomb Group.

One of only two flying Liberators left in the world is operated by the Collings Foundation. During World War II, this B-24J was flown in combat by the RAF. Afterwards, it became part of the Indian Air Force's bomber fleet. When the aircraft was restored in the 1980s, it was nicknamed *All American* in honour of a Fifteenth Air Force bomber with that moniker. The restored Liberator is seen all lit up during an evening event in 1990.

There are estimated to be over forty B-25s in airworthy condition worldwide. This B-25J was active on the air show scene in the US, but is currently based in Europe.

The B-24 known as *All American* made a series of low-level passes at Nellis Air Force Base in Nevada as part of a special air show to celebrate the 50th anniversary of the US Air Force. The Collings Foundation, which periodically altered aspects of the bomber's facade, later repainted its Liberator in the colours of an aircraft of the 64th Bomb Squadron, 43rd Bomb Group, which served in the Pacific theatre. It was nicknamed *Dragon and His Tail*. Later still, the paint scheme was changed with the aircraft currently sporting the nickname *Witchcraft*. The only other flyable Liberator is a B-24A, nicknamed *Ol' 927*, which is operated by the Commemorative Air Force of Midland, Texas. (*Photo by Philip Handleman*)

Because so many B-25Js were built and because they were the last of the major production models, more of them have survived than any other model of the Mitchell medium bomber. *Luck Lady* is reportedly now in storage in Virginia.

Reflecting the owner's personalization and Florida's renown as a natural habitat for alligators, this A-26 on display in the state features *Gator Invader* nose art.

Typical of the civil conversions is this A-26 seen taxiing at the Tico Air Show in Florida in 1990. The wing-tip fuel tanks and enlarged tail surfaces enabled greater range. Also, the interior was completely redone to accommodate passengers in executive comfort.

Most of the surviving Douglas A-26 Invaders were converted to executive transports when sold as war surplus. Occasionally, one outfitted like a World War II-era attack plane has graced air shows. In the early 1990s, an A-26 decked out in *Georgia Invader* nose art and with eight gun barrels protruding from the nose could be seen at flying events in south-eastern US.

The US supplied TBM-3s to Canada as well as other allies. Under the circumstances, it is quite fitting that there should be some restored examples proudly adorned in Canadian markings.

In general, the longevity of the big torpedo bomber is a tribute to its builders, Grumman and General Motors, as well as to its restorers and operators. This Canadian TBM-3 was pristine when it appeared on the air show scene nearly four decades after the war.

In 1944, the RAF transferred this and other photo-reconnaissance variants of the Mosquito to the US Army Air Forces. Some of the aircraft were used for highly classified special operations. This Mosquito PR.Mk XVI is pictured at Mount Farm, Oxfordshire.

Often overshadowed by its C-47 Army cousin, the US Navy's R4D provided invaluable service during and after World War II. Uses included radar countermeasures, air-sea warfare training, navigator training and general purpose transportation, among others. Not many Skytrains have been restored as Navy aircraft as is the case here.

The Naval Air Transport Service was created shortly after America's entry into the war and the R4D was the backbone of its operations. In total, the US Navy operated about 600 of the transports.

Philip Handleman with his US Navy Stearman biplane of World War II. (*Photo by Donald R. Sayles*)

Though large and weighing up to 65,000 pounds, the Avro Lancaster was praised by its pilots for fighter-like handling qualities. In this photograph, a Lanc is parked with its main wheels chocked and bomb bay doors swung open as a US soldier stands guard. Note the B-24 parked in the background to the right.

Powered by four Rolls-Royce Merlin engines (except for 300 aircraft that had the Bristol Hercules sleeve-valve radial engines), the Avro Lancaster was the RAF's leading heavy bomber during World War II. The aircraft was the mainstay of the night bombing campaign against Germany.

which entailed the installation of four of the reliable Rolls-Royce Merlin engines and the lengthening of the wing.

Initially called the Manchester III, this highly modified bomber took to the sky for the first time on 9 January 1941. A second test aircraft appeared in May, and it soon became evident that the changes resulted in spectacular performance. The big bomber's handling characteristics were synonymous with those of a fighter.

Orders were placed for the bomber, by now renamed the Lancaster. Because of the quantity desired, Avro's output was bolstered by production at Armstrong Whitworth, Austin Motors, and Vickers-Armstrong. The first of 3,425 production Lancaster Mk Is flew on 31 October 1941. Production aircraft differed from the prototypes in that they had the more powerful 1,620-horsepower Merlin XXIV engines.

Operational use began in early 1942. Throughout its service during the remainder of the war, the Lancaster performed with distinction. Its mammoth proportions enabled it to carry gigantic bombs, most notably the 22,000-lb Grand Slam, the heaviest single bomb of the war. For the type's most publicized mission, nineteen Lancasters were expressly modified to carry spinning, drum-like bombs designed by Barnes Wallis for the specialized task of destroying dams. On the night of 16/17 May 1943, the Lancasters of the RAF's newly formed No. 617 Squadron, under the command of Guy Gibson, struck Ruhr Valley dams and knocked out two of them. Gibson was awarded the Victoria Cross and the squadron became known as the 'Dam Busters.'

High-rate production of the Rolls-Royce Merlin engine was still not sufficient to satisfy demand. Accordingly, an alternative powerplant was selected for the Lancaster. The Mk II was powered by 1,735-horsepower Bristol Hercules VI air-cooled radial engines. These engines were reliable but did not offer the same cruise speed performance or the same fuel efficiency as the Merlin. This Lancaster model, which also differed from the original with the addition of a ventral gun turret, was cancelled after just 300 were produced.

The availability of US-built Packard Motor versions of the Rolls-Royce Merlin allowed Avro to go back to producing Lancasters with the preferred engine. A total of 3,039 Mk IIIs were built. They were essentially identical to the Mk Is except for the manufacturing origin of their engines.

Bomber Command's Lancasters made extensive use of the H2S ground-mapping radar. The device's presence was apparent in an aft underside blister. Some bombers also had the Gee-H precision navigational equipment. An array of additional electronics found application in other Lancasters, most notably with No. 100 Group which specialized in electronic countermeasure warfare. Other Lancasters were also used by Coastal Command in maritime patrol, anti-submarine, and air-sea rescue missions.

The Lancaster will for ever be remembered as the bomber that fulfilled RAF Bomber Command's requirement for mass night raids against German targets. In what remains a controversial strategy, the carpet bombing was carried out under the steely leadership of Air Chief Marshal Arthur 'Bomber' Harris. The doctrine was a concession to the belief of the British High Command that true precision bombing was not feasible and that night operations were the only way to maintain a modicum of safety for the bomber crews.

On some occasions a thousand bombers of various types were assembled in aerial armadas with the strikes occurring in waves. The first of these strikes, which included Lancasters from

No. 5 Group, occurred against Köln on 30/31 May 1942. Some of the European air war's most devastating raids were those that hit Hamburg from 24 July to 3 August 1943 and Dresden on 14 February 1945. Throughout the war, Lancasters flew 156,000 sorties, mostly against German targets, and dropped 618,273 tons of bombs.

Specifications (for Mk I)
Manufacturer A.V. Roe
Type: heavy bomber with crew of seven
Powerplant: four 1,640-horsepower Merlin XXIV liquid-cooled V-12 engines
Wingspan: 102 ft 0 in
Length: 69 ft 6 in
Height: 20 ft 0 in
Maximum take-off weight: 65,000 lb
Maximum speed: 287 miles per hour
Cruising speed: 227 miles per hour
Service ceiling: 24,500 ft
Range: 1,660 miles with 14,000-lb bomb load, 1,040 miles with 22,000-lb bomb load
Armament: ten 0.303-in machine guns, typically up to 14,000 lb of bombs

Mighty Citadel: Boeing B-17 Flying Fortress
Much of US air power doctrine in the pre-war years was embodied in the emerging heavy bomber that appropriately went by the name Flying Fortress. Though the aircraft was initially conceived as a defensive bomber whose primary mission would be the aerial interdiction of hostile ships approaching America's shores, as war loomed ever more ominously overseas the mission focus shifted to offensive operations. Leading American air power theorists believed with growing conviction that massed formations of fast heavy bombers, festooned with guns, would constitute an impenetrable mobile citadel.

In response to a 1934 Army Air Corps request for a 'multi-engined bomber,' Boeing engineers astonished many by choosing not a twin-engine but a four-engine configuration. On 28 July 1935, the Model 299 completed its first successful test flight. However, at flight trials later that year, the aircraft plummeted to the ground upon take-off in a tragic accident because someone had failed to remove the elevator locks. This setback caused programme delays, but the potential for the bomber was obvious and so a contract was issued for thirteen evaluation aircraft.

The US Navy felt threatened that its role in protecting America's shores might be usurped by the B-17 and did not look kindly upon the new bomber. This opposition notwithstanding, the Army ordered the first production B-17B. Its Wright Cyclone air-cooled radial engines had exhaust-driven superchargers. When the model entered service in 1939, it set the world's speed and altitude records for bombers.

The B-17C arrived in 1940 and a small number was promptly supplied to the British. Despite cautions voiced by American officers that this model was not yet ready for combat, the British plunged ahead with deployment. Predictably, many of the aircraft were destroyed. This left a discomfiting feeling about the B-17's prospects and put the Army Air Corps into a position of having to defend its decision to rely substantially on the Flying Fortress.

At the time of the Japanese attack on Pearl Harbor, the B-17D was on hand at both Hawaii and the Philippines. There wasn't much these bombers could do to reverse the situation in light of the stunning surprise and overwhelming enemy numbers. The next model, the B-17E, had enlarged tail surfaces for better control authority at high altitude plus it was more heavily armed. This model was the first of the type to have a production run in excess of 500.

On 17 August 1942, US Eighth Air Force commander, Ira C. Eaker, led the first US B-17 raid over Europe in an E model nicknamed *Yankee Doodle*. The B-17F soon followed, but it wasn't until the B-17G arrived at Eighth Air Force airfields in East Anglia that crews had the kind of heavy bomber originally envisaged by the air power theorists. The G model incorporated the lessons learned at great cost during the early air campaign. The most conspicuous change was the addition of a chin turret with twin 0.5-in machine guns to provide defensive fire against *Luftwaffe* interceptors that had exploited the frontal zone's vulnerability.

While B-17s were deployed to various theatres, it is the Eighth Air Force service that defined the bomber's contribution to the war effort. Courageous crews forged ahead, often amid heavy flak and swarms of interceptors, in an all-out drive to grind the German war machine to a halt. The doctrine called for daylight precision bombing through the employment of the Norden bombsight.

Although the raids were hardly precise by today's standards, the relentless manner in which they were pursued eventually led to serious degradation of the enemy's infrastructure, particularly its fuel supply. Until early 1944, when the beneficial effect of long-range fighter escorts took hold, the heavy bomber squadrons sustained alarming losses.

In accordance with the custom of bomber crews, this B-17F of the 547th Bomb Squadron, 384th Bomb Group, records its mission count on the aircraft's nose.

The hazards of air combat accompanied bomber crews throughout the war. Flak and interceptors posed mortal threats. The port wing of this B-17F has been shot away by an Me 262 over Crantenburg, Germany.

To a large extent, the Allied victory hinged on American industrial might's ability to keep large numbers of B-17s rolling off assembly lines, 12,731 in total. The vast quantity came from not only Boeing, but under licence from Douglas and Lockheed Vega. The continual inflow of new Flying Fortresses to overseas airfields maintained the 'aluminium overcast' that saturated the enemy and hastened the liberation of Europe.

Specifications (for B-17F)
Manufacturer: Boeing
Type: heavy bomber with crew of eight to ten
Powerplant: four 1,200-horsepower Wright R-1820-97 Cyclone radial piston engines
Wingspan: 103 ft 9 in
Length: 74 ft 9 in
Height: 19 ft 2 in
Maximum take-off weight: 72,000 lb (wartime full load)
Maximum speed: 295 miles per hour
Cruising speed: 160 miles per hour
Service ceiling: 36,000 ft
Range: 4,420 miles (typical 800-mile combat radius with bomb load)
Armament: twelve 0.5-in Browning machine guns, up to 17,600-lb bomb load

Flying Fortresses were amazingly resilient in the face of veritable brick walls of enemy fire. This B-17G of the 398th Bomb Group sustained a flak blast that destroyed its nose. Nevertheless, the crew returned the damaged aircraft to base.

Lumbering Giant: Consolidated B-24 Liberator

The story of the Liberator is almost equally as much a narrative of America's extraordinary wartime manufacturing clout. Never before or since were so many heavy bombers of a particular type constructed in so short a time. Though this heavy bomber did not have noticeably better performance than its American counterpart, the B-17, which derived from design concepts inaugurated five years earlier, it benefited from the urgency of bringing as many of the newest heavy bombers into service as rapidly as possible.

In 1944, the Liberator workforce peaked at more than 180,000, reflecting the scale of manufacturing. Production occurred at Consolidated Aircraft's origination plant in San Diego, a sister plant in Fort Worth, a nearby North American Aviation factory in Dallas, the Douglas facility in Tulsa, and Ford's Willow Run assembly line outside of Detroit. For a time, the Ford operation was managed by none other than Charles Lindbergh.

The massive four-engine bomber rolled out at some of these plants at an almost incomprehensible rate of one an hour. Total output came to an astounding 18,313. This was about 44 per cent higher than B-17 production and more than double the number of Lancasters built.

Design work began at Consolidated Aircraft in early 1939 and the Model 32 prototype flew before the end of the year. The aircraft was notable for its long-span Davis wing mounted above mid-fuselage, which offered a reduction in drag. Unlike most configurations of the time,

The first US Army version of the Liberator was the B-24A. Lightly armed, it was used mainly as a transport. Note the stars and stripes of the American flag decorating the nose.

it had tricycle landing gear. There were two large bomb bays in the chunky fuselage with a catwalk through the centre connecting fore and aft fuselage sections.

An interesting feature was the set of hydraulically operated bomb bay doors. They furled open and shut like the cover of a roll-top desk. The prototype was equipped with supercharged Pratt & Whitney Twin Wasp air-cooled radial engines, and later production models had turbo-superchargers to improve cruising speed at mission altitudes.

Among the first true production models was the LB-30, designated the Liberator Mk I by the RAF. Sent to Britain even before America's entry into the war, one was used as the personal transport of Prime Minister Winston Churchill. This special-purpose aircraft was called the *Commando*. Later in the war, Churchill's transport, though retaining the same name, became a single-finned version of the type like the US Navy's PB4Y patrol bomber or RY transport.

The first model that went into mass production was the B-24D. This aircraft incorporated refinements based on the experience of earlier, low-rate production models. Because of an approved gross weight of thirty tons, it ranked as the heaviest US aircraft up to that time.

The B-24D was ideally suited for long-range, over water missions because of its high-aspect-ratio wing design and fuel capacity. Thus, it served as a bomber in the Pacific theatre and as a maritime patrol platform in the North Atlantic where German submarines were a serious menace. The US Navy recognized the value of the Liberator and started taking delivery of the type in modified configuration in 1943, re-designating it the PB4Y-1 and renaming it the Privateer. The RAF used the Liberator in thirty-seven squadrons in all theatres.

The Liberator's load-carrying ability made it a worthy candidate for cargo/transport aircraft, and such models were built. Armament was removed and replaced with up to twenty seats along with space for up to five tons of cargo. The US Army version was the C-87 and the US Navy's equivalent was the RY.

Some Liberators were converted into aerial fuel trucks. These C-109 transports ferried almost three tons of vitally needed aviation fuel on each hop across the treacherous mountain range that separated Burma from China. Another derivative of the B-24D was the F-7, an early strategic photo-reconnaissance aircraft packed with eleven cameras.

Liberators are often associated with memorable raids on the oil fields and refineries near Ploesti, Romania. Since Germany relied heavily on these sources for fuel, the Allies targeted them early on. The first raid involved twelve B-24Ds from a special detachment on 11/12 June 1942. Little damage was inflicted on the target, so a larger raid involving 178 Liberators, called Operation *Tidal Wave*, was organized for 1 August 1943.

Although portions of the complex were disabled, the overall impact was disappointing. Raids continued until the spigot was turned off about a year later. Approximately 7,500 sorties

Part of the reason for Allied success in World War II was the mass production of vitally needed aircraft. No type better illustrates the point than the B-24. Because of ingenious assembly techniques combined with an unwavering patriotic spirit, 18,313 B-24s were produced. Some plants ratcheted up output to a completed bomber every hour.

were conducted with 13,500 tons of bombs dropped. The toll was incredibly high with 350 heavy bombers lost.

The B-24J was the next major model. It had a new autopilot and bombsight, and was outwardly distinguishable from the D model by the installation of a twin-gun nose turret. The aircraft's split-tail configuration had been determined to be less than optimal, but a redesign with the associated retooling was too onerous to be implemented in a timely fashion except for a quantity of the new US Navy PB4Y-1s. This model had an extremely tall fin/rudder and an elongated fuselage. It was intended for low-level maritime patrol, but most of these aircraft reached the operational inventory shortly after the war ended.

Specifications (for B-24D)
Manufacturer: Consolidated Aircraft
Type: heavy bomber with crew of ten
Powerplant: four 1,200-horsepower Pratt & Whitney R-1830-43 Twin Wasp radial piston engines
Wingspan: 110 ft 0 in
Length: 66 ft 4 in
Height: 17 ft 11 in
Maximum take-off weight: 60,000 lb
Maximum speed: 303 miles per hour
Cruising speed: 200 miles per hour
Service ceiling: 32,000 ft
Range: 2,850 miles (typical 1,080-mile combat radius with bomb load)
Armament: ten 0.5-in Browning machine guns, 8,800-lb bomb load

Remarkable Raider: North American B-25 Mitchell
Brigadier General William 'Billy' Mitchell was the US Army Air Service's most vociferous air power advocate dating back to his days commanding large combat formations during World War I. Mitchell's outspokenness repeatedly got him in trouble with his superiors. Though his ideas were sound, sometimes even prophetic, his methods never failed to infuriate.

By the mid-1920s, Mitchell's recalcitrance culminated in his court martial. Yet, as the years passed, many of his bold pronouncements regarding air warfare were vindicated. It was, therefore, not surprising that on the eve of World War II, when Mitchell's prescient concepts bore immediate relevance, one of the Army Air Corps' new bomber types was christened in his memory.

The NA-40 was North American Aviation's early attempt to satisfy an Air Corps requirement for a medium bomber. Modifications were made, most notably a switch from Pratt & Whitney engines to more powerful Wright engines. Re-engined, the prototype became the NA-40B. In a bid to supply Britain and France, the aircraft lost to a competing Douglas design. But, the NA-40B impressed US Army officials in flight tests.

Even though the prototype crashed on 11 April 1939, only two weeks after its evaluation had begun at Wright Field in Ohio, the US Army placed an order for the bomber. The first 184 aircraft were rushed through production and encompassed three models. The major design change to all aircraft after the first nine was to the wing.

Originally, a constant dihedral defined the wing, meaning that the wing was angled up from the root. This caused directional instability and was corrected by retaining the dihedral only between the fuselage and engine nacelles while the remainder of the wing was straightened outboard from the nacelles. This modification gave the B-25 its gull-wing appearance.

The most daring mission in the type was America's first retaliatory strike against Japan. On 18 April 1942, sixteen B-25B bombers launched from the USS *Hornet* under the lead of Lieutenant Colonel James H. 'Jimmy' Doolittle, an already famous air racing champion and accomplished test pilot. Known as the Doolittle Raiders, the mission's eighty volunteer pilots and crew were forced to take off from the heaving carrier deck a few hundred miles in advance of the planned start because of detection by an enemy picket boat.

The added distance meant they would not be able to reach improvised landing sites in China, prepared expressly for them, after their attacks on Tokyo, Kobe, Yokohama and Nagoya. Forced landings or bail outs were necessitated and amazingly almost all of the Raiders survived. The raid caused some damage to the targets, but the real value was in debunking the myth of Japan's invincibility.

From then on, Japan didn't know when it might be attacked. On the other side of the equation, the Allies got a needed morale boost. Doolittle was promptly promoted and upon his return home was awarded the Medal of Honor.

This is a North American Aviation B-25C which incorporated many improvements over the preceding model.

The most famous B-25 mission occurred on 18 April 1942. Then Lieutenant Colonel James H. 'Jimmy' Doolittle led a force of sixteen B-25B Mitchell bombers on the first air strike against Japan. The fully loaded Army medium bombers launched from the deck of the USS *Hornet*, a first in Army Air Forces and Navy history. Some of the B-25s are seen on the aircraft carrier's deck with their engine cowlings covered by tarpaulins.

Numerous models followed the early production models with the RAF receiving the second highest number after the Army Air Forces. A dizzying array of modifications was applied depending on the intended mission of the respective aircraft. The C and D models were identical to each other, but carried different identifiers because they were assembled in different plants. They had autopilots and attachments for external fuel tanks.

The B-25G carried the Army's 75-mm field gun in its nose for anti-shipping missions in the Pacific. The adaptation was not fruitful, however, and the company looked to the B-25H to rectify it. A lighter 75-mm cannon was installed along with four 0.5-in machine guns also in the nose and four more in 'side pockets'. Frontal firepower was enormous plus the aircraft could carry a 3,000-lb bomb load and eight five-inch rockets under the wings.

The main model was the B-25J. Initially, this model was built with the traditional bombardier's nose. However, experience revealed that medium bombers were not conducting high-level bomb runs. Rather, they were flying low-level ground attack missions. Under the circumstances, the aircraft were retro-fitted with eight 0.5-in machine guns in the nose, which combined with ten other machine guns on board to make the aircraft a formidable weapons platform. An unarmed photo-reconnaissance model, known as the F-10, was produced starting in 1943.

The third largest quantity of B-25s went to the US Navy which used the designation PBJ. Deliveries started in 1943 with a Marine squadron receiving the first ones. Many other countries flew the Mitchell in a plethora of duties, which reflected the prudence of the type's underlying design as well as its adaptability.

Later, some Mitchells were used by the Army Air Forces as pilot and navigator trainers. The Air Force continued this use until January 1959. In the post-war years, these aircraft were executive transports, fire-bombers, camera platforms, and even crop dusters. A total of 9,816 were built, more than any other US medium bomber.

Specifications (for B-25D)
Manufacturer: North American Aviation
Type: medium bomber with crew of five
Powerplant: two 1,700-horsepower Wright R-2600-13 14-cylinder radial piston engines
Wingspan: 67 ft 7 in
Length: 52 ft 11 in
Height: 15 ft 10 in
Maximum take-off weight: 35,000 lb
Maximum speed: 284 miles per hour
Cruising speed: 233 miles per hour
Service ceiling: 21,200 ft
Range: 1,500 miles
Armament: two 0.5-in machine guns in nose, twin 0.5-in machine guns in each dorsal and retractable ventral turrets, up to 3,000 lb of bombs

Assault Machine: Martin B-26 Marauder
The Glenn L. Martin Company's Peyton M. Magruder made a valiant attempt to push the state of the art in the US Army Air Corps medium bomber competition of the late 1930s. On paper and in appearance his creation seemed to hold great promise. The Model 179, as it was then known, exuded a sense of advancement as though it somehow had leapfrogged half a generation ahead. With its circular fuselage and pointy nose, it stood apart from the other twin-engine aircraft of the time, as if giving a tease of the aviation future.

The Army Air Corps was so taken by the drawings and performance estimates, that it placed an order based on them alone. First flight occurred on 25 November 1940. Indeed, in keeping with the positive impression, the first production models exceeded 300 miles per hour. But there was a trade-off. The wing area was relatively limited, which meant that the aircraft had a high wing loading. In fact, it was the highest wing loading of any aircraft in the US Army.

As a result, the B-26 had tricky handling characteristics with potentially dangerous ramifications, especially when manoeuvring at low speeds close to the ground such as when taking off or landing. Moreover, touchdown speed was nearly 100 miles per hour, unusually fast for an aircraft of that era.

Flight training occurred at MacDill Field in Tampa, Florida, and the accident rate was so high that people in the area remarked 'One a day in Tampa Bay'. At one point, production was suspended and an inquiry convened to examine the aircraft's safety. Changes were recommended and the programme resumed.

Beginning with a sub-variant of the B-26B, the wing was lengthened by six feet which increased wing area. However, at the same time, aircraft weight rose, which hampered the objective. Wing incidence was deficient and the nose-wheel strut was lengthened in an attempt to improve this factor. It wasn't until later models that the troublesome wing incidence was addressed *per se* with an increase of 3.5 degrees. This improved take-off and landing qualities, but at the same time there was a sacrifice in maximum speed.

'One a day in Tampa Bay' was the derisive comment on the Martin B-26 Marauder in connection with its tricky handling characteristics that resulted in a number of the aircraft falling in the waters near the Tampa, Florida, training base. Once the medium bomber's peculiarities were mastered, it became an effective instrument in the air war.

The B-26G was the last consequential production model in the Marauder series. Design improvements included a higher wing incidence.

After a rough break-in period, the Marauder found its niche and crews developed respect for the bomber. Avoiding the aircraft's pitfalls and realizing its potential came down to knowing the unique shortcomings and simply dealing with them on daily missions. The Marauder ended up with the lowest loss rate of any US Army Air Forces bomber in the European theatre.

The B-26 went first to the Pacific where it flew missions over New Guinea, wielded torpedoes at Midway and attacked enemy ships in the Aleutians. By late 1942, B-26 squadrons were in North Africa and continued to support troops pushing across the Mediterranean and into Italy. In 1943, the type was deployed to northern Europe where enemy ground fire plagued low-level formations. The aircraft were vulnerable to intense flak.

In November 1943, the nucleus of the newly activated Ninth Air Force took shape in England, comprising tactical assets of Eighth Air Force. In this organization, which aimed to support Allied ground forces in connection with the upcoming invasion of the continent, the B-26 demonstrated its strengths. Applying the lessons of earlier missions over Europe, the B-26s flew missions at medium altitudes and with fighter escort.

The Marauder entered service with the RAF and the South African Air Force. The remaining variants after the C model were not built in great quantity, though the F and G models had the higher-incidence wing. Some B and C models were converted into AT-23 trainers. Also, the Navy and Marine Corps used some JM conversions as target tugs.

Production ended as the war drew to a close. The total number built was 5,157. The Marauder was phased out of Air Force service in 1948 and the type designation transferred to the Douglas A-26 Invader.

Specifications (for B-26B)
Manufacturer: Martin
Type: medium bomber with crew of seven
Powerplant: two 1,920-horsepower Pratt & Whitney R-2800-43 radial piston engines
Wingspan: 71 ft 0 in
Length: 58 ft 3 in
Height: 21 ft 6 in
Maximum take-off weight: 37,000 lb
Maximum speed: 317 miles per hour
Cruising speed: 260 miles per hour
Service ceiling: 23,500 ft
Range: 1,150 miles
Armament: one 0.3-in machine gun each in nose and ventral tunnel or two 0.5-in beam machine guns in lieu of tunnel gun, two 0.5-in machine guns each in tail and dorsal turrets, up to 5,200 lb in bombs or torpedoes

Knockout Puncher: Boeing B-29 Superfortress

Boeing's Superfortress was aptly named. The B-29 emerged as one of the greatest engineering feats of World War II. The enormity of the task was overwhelming and destined to take more than six years from first tentative steps to operational readiness. Without the vision of both Army Air Corps officers and company executives in the 1930s, this weapon that ultimately assured victory might not have been available in time.

In October 1938, the Army Air Corps announced a requirement for a replacement of the B-17 which was itself suffering from Congressional penny-pinching at that very time. The performance specifications set out for the replacement bomber were so prodigious one wonders if those responsible for promulgating them and those charged with delivering on them really believed they were attainable. Armed with a determination equal to the audacity of the challenge, the military/company team pressed state-of-the-art technology to the edge of the proverbial envelope to grasp the elusive goal.

The cigar-shaped B-29 had a glazed bombardier's nose. Fore and aft pressurized crew cabins were connected by a sealed tunnel. The two bomb bays utilized a release mechanism that dropped bombs alternately from each bay so as to maintain the centre of gravity. Wing loading was a problem. The aircraft when fully loaded weighed an astounding sixty-two tons. To bring landing speed to within manageable margins, Fowler flaps were installed on the wing trailing edges which, when extended, increased wing area by a sizable 21 per cent.

There were four remotely-operated gun turrets, each with two 0.5-in machine guns. A fifth turret was in the tail and it consisted of either two 0.5-in machine guns or a combination of two 0.5-in machine guns and a 20-mm cannon. The bomb load could be as much as 20,000 pounds.

Power came from four 2,200-horsepower Wright R-3350 Duplex Cyclone turbo-super-charged eighteen-cylinder radial piston engines. Each engine was encased in a nacelle that had to accommodate dual General Electric turbo-superchargers. The nacelles were built by Fisher Body Division of General Motors in Cleveland.

The aircraft were produced in four locations: Boeing's new assembly facility in Wichita, Kansas; the unused Sea Ranger building in Renton, Washington, which Boeing managed; the

When the Boeing B-29 Superfortress finally reached front-line squadrons, it was poised to advance the Asian air war. The world had never seen a bomber like this. It could fly faster, carry a heavier load and cover greater distance than any other heavy bomber up to that time.

Martin factory in Omaha, Nebraska; and the Bell plant in Marietta, Georgia. Altogether, 3,960 B-29s were built.

The first B-29 flew on 21 September 1942. Many 'bugs' had to be ironed out. Engine cooling problems, excessive fuel burn, and crew coordination needed lots of work. The Superfortress was a highly complicated aircraft and it took time to integrate it into the service that had never operated anything like it.

The first B-29 combat mission involved a small formation flying out of India which bombed the railroad marshalling yards in Bangkok on 5 June 1944. Ten days later, missions against Japan were commenced from bases in China. Fuel had to be ferried in for these missions 'over the Hump' from Burma. In November, the newly won islands of Tinian, Saipan and Guam were ready as launching points with newly constructed runways. As more B-29s arrived from the factories, the missions increased.

The newly formed Twentieth Air Force mounted raids unremittingly. The brash commander of XXI Bomber Command, Major General Curtis LeMay, decided to change tactics. Instead of high-level raids in which bombs were prone to stray because of exposure to strong winds, his bombers would fly at low altitude and strike Tokyo at night.

The B-29s peppered the city with incendiaries. Owing in part to the flimsy construction of homes in the city, firestorms erupted. On 9 March 1945, ordnance from waves of B-29s

B-29s of the 468th Bomb Group unload bombs on Rangoon, Burma.

scorched more than fifteen square miles and killed upwards of 80,000 people, which by some estimates was a greater death toll than that caused by the later atomic bombs.

On 6 August 1945, Colonel Paul Tibbets piloted his B-29, the *Enola Gay*, carrying a nuclear weapon to be used against a belligerent for the first time in history. The 20-kiloton *Little Boy* devastated the city of Hiroshima. Three days later a second bomb, employing a different technology and called *Fat Man*, was dropped by the B-29 *Bock's Car* on Nagasaki. In five more days the war came to a close.

Specifications (for B-29)
Manufacturer: Boeing
Type: heavy bomber with crew of ten
Powerplant: four turbocharged 2,200-horsepower Wright R-3350-23-23A/-41 Cyclone 18-cylinder radial piston engines
Wingspan: 141 ft 3 in
Length: 99 ft 0 in
Height: 29 ft 7 in
Maximum take-off weight: 124,000 lb
Maximum speed: 358 miles per hour
Cruising speed: 230 miles per hour

Service ceiling: 31,850 ft

Range: 3,250 miles

Armament: two 0.5-in machine guns in each of four remote controlled turrets, three 0.5-in machine guns or two 0.5-in machine guns and one 20-mm cannon in the tail turret, up to 20,000 lb of bombs

Mayhem Maker: Douglas A-20 Havoc

In the years immediately preceding World War II, Douglas Aircraft employed a wealth of designer talent. The company's design shop was a hotbed of activity with several outstanding professionals destined for renown within the industry. John K. 'Jack' Northrop (later to found his own firm) and Edward Heinemann conceived a simple twin-engine attack aircraft, known as the Model 7B. Regrettably, their one-off creation went down in an accident on 23 January 1939, a mere three months after its first flight.

The underlying design was sound, and the two design experts refined it with a shoulder-wing and a narrow-width but deep fuselage to arrive at the DB-7 (DB representing Douglas Bomber). Orders were placed by the US Army Air Corps, the French *Armée de l'Air*, and the RAF. The Soviet Union eventually received the type, as well. Known as the A-20 Havoc in Army use, the foreign air forces sometimes adopted the company designation with the nickname of Boston.

The initial batch of British aircraft was converted to night fighters. These retained the A-20 designation and Havoc title though other names were loosely applied. Armament for this duty consisted of four under-the-nose 0.303-in machine guns as well as a gun in the rear of the dorsal hump. Later, radar-equipped models had twelve nose-mounted machine guns. An American night fighter version was developed, designated the P-70.

Another modification was the placement in the nose of a searchlight with an enormous candlepower rating. The idea was that the illuminating aircraft, called the Havoc Mk II Turbinlite, would shine its light on an enemy aircraft so that accompanying Hurricanes could shoot it down. The scheme proved impractical.

The first American air combat mission in Europe was flown by members of the 15th Bomb Squadron in twelve borrowed Boston Mk IIICs of the RAF's No. 226 Squadron. Fittingly, the date was 4 July 1942. US Army A-20Cs soon thereafter conducted missions over Europe and later North Africa and Italy. The A-20G replaced these aircraft, the distinguishing feature of the new models was that their glazed glass noses were changed to accommodate half a dozen nose-mounted 0.5-in machine guns.

The A-20H had the more powerful 1,700-horsepower Wright Double Cyclone R-2600-29 engine. The last major models, the A-20J and A-20K, returned to the glazed nose. The latter of these was used to lead large formations of G and H models on bombing raids, providing the cue for when to release bombs. A small number of J and K models were converted into F-3A photo-reconnaissance aircraft.

The Havoc/Boston was a highly adaptable aircraft that performed ably in virtually all theatres and in many roles. Pilots liked its handling ease, initial climb rate, and visibility. Some aircraft were outfitted with a backup flight control system, enabling the radio operator/gunner in the aft cockpit to land if the lone pilot became incapacitated. The assembly lines churning out these aircraft stopped Havoc/Boston production in the autumn of 1944 as there were more modern aircraft being produced by then, notably Douglas' own follow-on attack plane. Total production was 7,525 units.

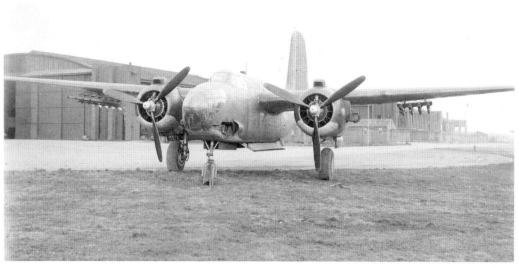

The RAF operated the Douglas A-20 Havoc. This is an RAF model, known as the DB-7 Boston Mk III. Note the rocket launchers on the outboard wings.

Maintaining a tight, multi-tiered formation, Ninth Air Force A-20Gs or A-20Hs roam over France. Earlier models featured a glazed nose. These aircraft concentrated up to six 0.5-in machine guns in a solid nose.

Specifications (for A-20G)
Manufacturer: Douglas Aircraft
Type: light attack bomber with crew of three
Powerplant: two 1,600-horsepower Wright R-2600-23 Double Cyclone radial piston engines
Wingspan: 61 ft 4 in
Length: 48 ft 0 in
Height: 17 ft 7 in
Maximum take-off weight: 27,200 lb
Maximum speed: 339 miles per hour
Cruising speed: 272 miles per hour
Service ceiling: 25,800 ft
Range: 1,090 miles
Armament: six nose-mounted 0.5-in machine guns, two 0.5-in machine guns in the dorsal turret, one 0.5-in machine gun in the ventral position, up to 4,000 lb of bombs

Mud Runner: Douglas A-26 Invader

The Invader was the replacement for the Havoc/Boston. Douglas Aircraft's design chief on the new attack plane project, Ed Heinemann, strove to incorporate the lessons learned from the real-world experience of the company's prior attack plane, which he had helped to shape. The result was an upscaled form of the earlier aircraft with more power and a preplanned architecture for multiple roles.

The new attack plane's wingspan was about nine feet longer than its predecessor. Length and height were nominally greater. The A-26 was powered by two 2,000-horsepower Pratt & Whitney R-2800-79 Double Wasp radial piston engines, representing an increase of 300 horsepower per engine over the last major A-20 model.

Given the variety of roles imposed on the Havoc, it was decided to make the A-26 ready for each mission category from the introduction of the type. Heinemann's team offered three basic versions: night fighter, ground attacker and level bomber.

It turned out that there was no demand for the A-26A night fighter, which had been designed to accommodate an airborne radar along with four 20-mm cannon in a ventral turret. By this time, Northrop was well into perfecting its mission-specific P-61.

The A-26B ground attack model was the most numerous produced with 1,355 entering service. This aircraft's nose was fitted with six and later eight 0.5-in machine guns. Remotely operated upper and lower turrets each had twin 0.5-in machine guns. The number of 0.5-in machine guns could be doubled with the addition of wing and fuselage packs.

A more traditional bomber configuration characterized the A-26C. It had a bombardier-type nose with a glazed finish. The bomb load was 4,000 pounds. The aircraft also had twin 0.5-in machine guns in the nose as well as in dorsal and ventral turrets.

The A-26 prototype flew for the first time on 10 July 1942, just six days after the A-20 had had its baptism of fire in Europe. Production models of the Invader started to reach the front in September 1944. As is often the case with follow-on equipment, the operators of the tried and true originals have a comfort level that is hard for the new version to match until enough time passes.

The issue was accentuated with the A-26 because upon its entry into the operational inventory it had some minor glitches that needed to be ironed out. Once the technical matters were addressed and as crews accumulated more flight time in the type, the Invader was increasingly recognized for its virtues. It manoeuvred well and the B model could achieve 355 miles per hour, the fastest speed of any US bomber during the war.

For the last two years of the war the A-26 increasingly supplanted the earlier A-20 and B-25 twin-engine attack planes/bombers. A-26s struck German targets from airfields in England, France and Italy. Most of the C model production went to the Pacific theatre. Missions were carried out against Formosa (Taiwan), Okinawa and Japan.

The Douglas plants in Long Beach, California, and Tulsa, Oklahoma, made Invaders over a comparatively short time reflecting the fact that the type did not enter the fray until the war was well under way. When the Martin B-26 Marauder was stricken from the operational roster a few years after the war, the A-26 assumed the Marauder's designation.

Pending orders for more than 5,250 A-26s were cancelled at war's end. Yet, Invaders were used in the Korean War where they remained highly regarded in the ground-attack role. In the 1960s, Invaders reconfigured as counterinsurgency aircraft were employed in South East Asia. In civilian hands, some Invaders were converted to executive transports because of the impressive speed and range.

Specifications (for A-26C)
Manufacturer: Douglas Aircraft
Type: light attack bomber with crew of three
Powerplant: two 2,000-horsepower Pratt & Whitney R-2800-79 Double Wasp radial piston engines
Wingspan: 70 ft 0 in
Length: 51 ft 3 in
Height: 18 ft 3 in
Maximum take-off weight: 35,000 lb
Maximum speed: 373 miles per hour
Cruising speed: 284 miles per hour
Service ceiling: 22,100 ft
Range: 1,400 miles
Armament: two 0.5-in machine guns each in the nose, dorsal position, and ventral position, up to 4,000 lb of bombs

Dive-bombing Diva: Douglas SBD Dauntless

The Dauntless was the right aircraft at the right place and at the right time. The type had been conceived by Jack Northrop as the BT-1 dive-bomber. Northrop's fledgling company became a division of Douglas Aircraft and in 1938, after Northrop himself left to venture out on his own again, the test article, designated the XBT-2, got a complete makeover. The brilliant Ed Heinemann led the masterful effort that resulted in the perfectly proportioned SBD (Scout Bomber Douglas).

The US Navy ordered the first production model on 8 April 1939. While the SBD was derided in some quarters as inadequate in speed, range and survivability, it proved itself

The Douglas SBD Dauntless dive-bomber is considered the best naval attack aircraft in some quarters. Though it was already approaching antiquated status early in the war, it provided the essential dive-bombing capability when it mattered. It will always be remembered as the aircraft that delivered the knockout blow against the Japanese fleet at Midway.

indisputably when put to the real-world test. At the Battle of the Coral Sea on 7 May 1942 and to an even greater extent at the decisive Battle of Midway on 4 June, Dauntlesses delivered crowning blows to the Japanese fleet.

In the first of these two engagements, SBDs sank the Japanese aircraft carrier *Shoho*. This was the first naval engagement in which the combatant ships fought against each other at distances that kept them out of visual range. Though the battle was not conclusive, it set the stage for the next encounter.

At Midway, antiquated Douglas TBD torpedo bombers threw themselves at the Japanese armada, slowly skimming in over the water. They were sitting ducks and most were wiped out. Yet, as the Japanese were focused on the low-level action, SBDs streamed down in classic dive-bombing runs and within just six minutes three of the Japanese carriers, *Akagi*, *Kaga* and *Soryu*, were aflame and on their way to the bottom of the ocean. A little later, the *Hiryu*, a fourth Japanese carrier, met the same fate.

By the end of that day, the course of the Pacific war, and arguably the entire war, had been reversed. The Battle of Midway was the American Battle of Britain for even though it did not occur over the homeland or last for months, it had everything hanging in the balance with a handful of courageous aircrewmen and their amazing aircraft determining the outcome.

The Dauntless had a greenhouse-type canopy which afforded good visibility for both the pilot in front and the gunner in the rear. The most distinctive design feature was the 'Swiss cheese' dive flaps/dive brakes. These split perforated surfaces, half of which opened above the wing and half below the wing, were deployed during steep dives to prevent excessive speed build-up and any structural damage. Though the SBD was relatively slow with a maximum speed of 255 miles per hour and a cruise speed of less than 200 miles per hour, its sturdy all-metal construction helped it to withstand battle damage and to return to its mother ship.

There were six major US Navy/Marine production models with changes from one to the next involving such items as electrical system upgrades, instrumentation enhancements and more powerful engines. The US Army Air Forces acquired the type and designated it the A-24. Nicknamed the Banshee in Army service, these dive-bombers went into combat in Indonesia, New Guinea and the Gilbert Islands. However, they did not match the results obtained by US Navy crews, suggesting that differences in training, tactics and basing may have accounted for the variance.

The service of SBDs in the North African and Atlantic campaigns has not received as much attention as the Pacific action, but the contributions were no less important. The US Navy dive-bombers provided support during Operation *Torch*, the Anglo-American amphibious

Three Dauntlesses from VC-24 in July 1943 provide a good view of the 'Swiss cheese' dive flaps. This design feature was critical to enabling the SBD's success in its assigned mission as a dive-bomber.

landings in Morocco and Algeria in early November 1942. Dauntlesses from the USS *Ranger* scored hits against Vichy French positions, helping to secure the Allies' advance. Nearly a year later, SBDs from the *Ranger* successfully attacked shipping in and around the harbour of Bodø on the Norwegian coast.

For its part, the Dauntless was able to achieve a high degree of accuracy through the dive-bombing techniques of the US Navy. Indeed, the Dauntless sank more tonnage of Japanese shipping than any other aircraft. Douglas built a total of 5,936.

Specifications (for SBD-5)
Manufacturer: Douglas Aircraft
Type: two-seat carrier-borne scout and dive bomber
Powerplant: one 1,200-horsepower Wright R-1820-60 Cyclone air-cooled radial piston engine
Wingspan: 41 ft 6½ in
Length: 33 ft 1½ in
Height: 13 ft 7 in
Maximum take-off weight: 10,700 lb
Maximum speed: 252 miles per hour
Cruising speed: 139 miles per hour
Service ceiling: 26,100 ft
Range: 1,115 miles with bomb load, 1,565 miles on reconnaissance mission
Armament: two 0.5-in machine guns in the nose, two 0.3-in machine guns in rear cockpit position, up to 1,600 lb of bombs under the fuselage, up to 650 lb of bombs under the wings

Big-Barrelled Besieger: Grumman TBF Avenger
When America entered World War II, its main in-service naval torpedo bomber was woefully outdated. The Douglas TBD, an all-metal monoplane, represented a provisional advance in the post-biplane era. As a mid-1930s design it lacked the performance required to be survivable let alone competitive in the next decade's war.

Fortunately, the need for a new aircraft to fill the void was recognized and by December 1940 the US Navy had selected a Grumman proposal right off the drawing board. The company's new TBF design was predicated on a new class of massive air-cooled radial engine. The leap in power from the TBD's 900-horsepower engine to the TBF's 1,700-horsepower (later the even higher 1,900-horsepower) engine was the key to improving performance.

In keeping with some other Grumman wartime designs of carrier-borne aircraft, the TBF was of monstrous proportions. The theory was that sheer power in the form of a big-barrelled air-cooled radial engine trumped the aerodynamic streamlining one might attain through use of a liquid-cooled engine. Moreover, the reliability and serviceability of a radial made it preferable, especially at sea, compared with the sometimes temperamental inline engines that bore an inherent vulnerability to radiator coolant leaks from enemy fire.

The TBF's all-metal fuselage was a deep-chested oval shape with a greenhouse-style canopy defined in the rear by an electrically controlled spherical turret. The lower aft fuselage had a compartment for a bombardier/gunner. The area forward of this position was allocated to storage and a voluminous weapons bay.

A landing signal officer guides the pilot of an inbound TBM on approach to landing aboard a US Navy aircraft carrier. Note the extended tailhook.

The wings had a rectangular centre section and equally tapered outboard sections. The span of over 54 feet did much to control wing loading and gave the aircraft good handling qualities, but necessitated a practical folding mechanism for deck and bay storage. Part of the aircraft's design genius was manifested in the hydraulically powered wing folding with patented skewed hinges that brought the outer wing section to sit sideways along the fuselage.

With a mid-wing configuration, the main landing gear required long legs. Grumman built these to be exceptionally strong. They were rated to withstand a teeth-shattering sink rate of 16 feet per second. Because this strength and durability was built into Grumman products, the company earned praise as the 'Iron Works'.

By coincidence, the company unveiled its first two prototypes in a formal ceremony at its Bethpage, Long Island, plant on 7 December 1941. Word reached executives that Pearl Harbor had been attacked. From that moment, the TBF was known as the Avenger. It should be noted

This TBF of VT-51 was photographed in July 1944 operating from the USS *San Jacinto*. During World War II, former president, George H.W. Bush, was a TBF pilot assigned to the same aircraft carrier.

that the British, who over time received nearly 1,000 of these aircraft, initially adopted the name Tarpon, but reverted back to the original American name before long.

New torpedo bombers were desperately needed at the front, and to meet the demand arrangements were made for General Motors to supplement Grumman's output. The giant auto company had plants in New Jersey, New York and Maryland that were running at less than capacity, so these were lumped into what the company called its Eastern Division. Proving that auto assembly line techniques had tremendous application to aircraft production, the Eastern Division built 7,546 Avengers, which was far more than the number produced by Grumman. Using the US Navy's letter identification code for manufacturers, the acronym for these aircraft changed to TBM with General Motors represented by the 'M.'

The aircraft's first combat engagement raised doubts about the type's viability. On 4 June 1942, a detachment of six TBFs belonging to VT-8 took off from Midway to attack Japanese warships sighted approximately 150 miles to the north-west. Like the battle's obsolete TBDs, the just deployed TBFs were badly shot up.

Only one Avenger survived the ordeal. Piloted by Ensign Albert K. 'Bert' Earnest, that aircraft's main elevator control linkage was severed by enemy fire. As Earnest turned his elevator trim wheel to the nose-up position by force of habit during approach to landing since a ditching in the water seemed imminent, he realized that he had pitch authority after all. The trim control linkage was intact because it was designed as a redundant system. Earnest continued his torpedo run against one of the ships and then turned back to Midway.

Despite the Avenger's dismaying combat debut, with changes in tactics the type proved to be effective. A nagging reliability problem with American air-launched torpedoes, though, impinged on the Avenger's offensive capability until the deficiency was corrected later in the war. The aircraft could drop four 500-pound bombs instead of a torpedo. In addition, eight 60-pound rockets could be carried under the wing. With the TBF-3, armament was bolstered by two forward-firing 0.5-in machine guns whereas there had been only a single 0.3-in gun before.

Altogether, the 9,836 Avengers produced during the war constituted more than twenty models and sub-variants. With the TBF-3E the US Navy obtained its first specialized carrier-borne anti-submarine warfare aircraft, which was outfitted with the RT-5/APS-4 radar and associated pod under the starboard wing. The major post-war development was the TBF-3W, which served as an airborne early warning (AEW) platform. It utilized the APS-20 surveillance radar with sensor equipment located in a large belly radome. In civilian hands after the war, Avengers were used extensively for firefighting and crop-dusting.

Specifications (for TBF-1)
Manufacturer: Grumman
Type: three-seat carrier-borne torpedo bomber
Powerplant: one 1,700-horsepower Wright R-2600-8 Cyclone double-row 14-cylinder radial piston engine
Wingspan: 54 ft 2 in
Length: 40 ft 0 in
Height: 16 ft 5 in
Maximum take-off weight: 17,364 lb
Maximum speed: 271 miles per hour
Cruising speed: 145 miles per hour
Service ceiling: 22,400 ft
Range: 1,105 miles
Armament: one nose-mounted 0.3-in machine gun, one 0.5-in machine gun in top turret, one 0.3-in machine gun in ventral position, one 22.7-in torpedo or up to 1,600 lb of bombs

Temperamental Beast: Curtiss SB2C Helldiver
Even before the prototype made its maiden flight on 18 December 1940, hopes were high that the newest Helldiver in the long line of Curtiss-Wright aircraft to use that appellation would perform in keeping with the proud tradition. It was also anticipated that this emerging aircraft would be a worthy replacement for the Douglas Dauntless, another dive-bomber based on an earlier design. Yet, almost from the beginning of the flight test programme, the addition to the Helldiver pedigree demonstrated a problematic streak that stigmatized it throughout the remainder of the war.

The Helldiver had an accentuated arch in the tail section along with a tall, rounded rudder that gave the aircraft a primal appearance as though it belonged more to the pre-war era than to the emerging vanguard of modern high-performance combat planes. It was as if the Curtiss design team had a fixation on these features for they had been incorporated in the company's predecessor design, the SBC biplane of 1933 vintage. Also, the rounded rudder was a prominent feature of the company's pre-war P-40 and of its precursor, the P-36.

On 8 February 1941, the sole XSB2C-1 prototype crashed on landing. During the prototype's rebuilding, many design changes occurred in an attempt to correct a litany of problems from stability deficiencies to troubling stall characteristics. However, on 21 December 1941, only two months after the prototype resumed flying, it came apart during flight. Thankfully, the test pilot baled out safely, but the project fell even further behind.

A year later, the company managed to deliver production SB2C-1 Helldivers to a US Navy squadron for the first time. These aircraft incorporated design changes required by the quirks discerned in the testing, but weight increased substantially without an engine upgrade, which, in turn, hindered performance. Other problems remained such as violent buffeting during high-speed dives. The lingering defects would have to be addressed with modifications to later models.

Though known as the 'Beast' because of its troublesome ways, the Helldiver could be mastered. These aircraft belong to the 4th Marine Air Wing and are shown over the central Pacific, having launched from a base in the Marshall Islands.

In a genuine action photograph snapped by Captain Robert Wood, SB2C-1s of VB-17 are seen entering the traffic pattern of the USS *Bunker Hill* following a raid on Rabaul on 11 November 1943. The arrester hook is down and soon the landing gear will be extended.

Harry S. Truman, then a US senator, oversaw investigations into questionable defence contractor practices and specifically looked into the Curtiss dive-bomber project. His committee issued a critical report. The Congressional findings caused most of the US Army's order for the aircraft, to be known as the A-25 Shrike, to be diverted to other customers.

The Helldiver finally went into action on 11 November 1943 when crews of VB-17 participated in raids on the Japanese stronghold at Rabaul on the island of New Britain. From that point, the Helldiver gradually gained a footing in the Pacific air war. The problems, however, did not stop arising. There were in-flight breakups and landing calamities on carrier decks.

The record was mixed. Some crews developed a rapport with the aircraft while others disdained it. In any case, Helldivers replaced more and more SBDs, and, despite ongoing technical troubles, carved out a niche as dive-bombers that could be efficaciously operated in combat if pilots remained fully cognizant of the aircraft's numerous and prominent idiosyncrasies.

Incremental improvements were made for the remainder of the war, more than 800 design changes in all. Many corresponded to new model introductions. For example, with the SB2C-3 an engine with a higher horsepower rating was installed. With the SB2C-4 came perforated upper wing dive brakes and lower wing dive flaps. The notorious tail buffeting experienced in steep dives was partially abated by this new feature. Appearing about a year before VJ Day, the -4 was built in greater numbers than any other Helldiver model.

Reflecting the difficulties presented by the Helldiver, many people referred to it sardonically as the 'Beast'. The aircraft's actual performance fell short of expectations, but it would not be accurate to write off the dive-bomber as a dud or deathtrap. The solution to successful operation hinged on understanding how to harness the ornery bronco. By war's end, more than 7,200 Helldivers had been produced, but, tellingly, they were the last aircraft Curtiss built for the US Navy.

Specifications (for SB2C-3)

Manufacturer: Curtiss-Wright
Type: two-seat carrier-borne scout bomber
Powerplant: one 1,900-horsepower Wright R-2600-20 Cyclone double-row 14-cylinder radial piston engine
Wingspan: 49 ft 8¾ in
Length: 36 ft 8 in
Height: 14 ft 9 in
Maximum take-off weight: 16,750 lb
Maximum speed: 293 miles per hour
Cruising speed: 158 miles per hour
Service ceiling: 26,700 ft
Range: 1,200 miles
Armament: two wing-mounted 20-mm cannon, two 0.3-in machine guns in rear cockpit position, one Mk 13-2 torpedo or up to 2,000 lb of bombs in bay or two 500-lb bombs under wings

Dumbo: Consolidated PBY Catalina

Unlikely as it may seem, the PBY was a wartime success even though it was among the oldest and slowest aircraft in service during the conflict. Based on Consolidated's earlier P2Y flying boat, the prototype PBY, known as the XP3Y-1, first flew on 28 March 1935. The PBY did not appear in an amphibian version until much later.

Because of its bomb-carrying capacity, the production model was re-designated PBY-1 to denote its patrol bomber status. The 'Y' stood for the manufacturer under the US Navy's code system. The first PBY-1s entered operational service with the US Navy's VP-11F in October 1936.

The PBY's longevity was related to the straightforwardness of its design, ease of handling, serviceability, relatively low cost and all-around practicality. These factors tended to compensate for the aircraft's tortoise-like movement in cruise flight. Of course, freedom to roam the sky depended in large measure on keeping the hostile air forces at bay. If enemy fighters had not been under threat of Allied fighters, the PBYs would have been far more susceptible to interception.

Conceived as a rugged sea-based workhorse, the PBY was of all-metal construction other than a few small sections like the ailerons which were fabric-covered. The high-wing was semi-cantilevered, strut-braced and pylon-mounted. Fascinatingly, the outboard floats retracted into the edges of the wing to form the wing tips. A spacious cockpit offered a comfortable environment for the pilot and co-pilot on missions that could last roughly a whole day. A glass-encased turret sat atop the stepped-down bow just below the cockpit crew's line of sight. There were also sliding side panels for the waist gunner positions, which incorporated bulging glass blisters in later models.

The aircraft was highly regarded and the British ordered 200 on 20 December 1939. Orders continued to stream in and most went to Coastal Command. In British service the flying boat was called the Catalina and the US Navy adopted the nickname.

Canada, too, wanted this aircraft and arrangements were made for supplemental production to occur at Canadian Vickers and Boeing-Vancouver. In Royal Canadian Air Force service the PBY was called the Canso. The Soviets were among the first to recognize the value of these long-range flying boats and began building them under licence.

Even the earliest Catalina production model was a remarkably efficient flying boat. This PBY-1 was photographed patrolling over Alaska in the pre-war years.

The PBY-1 set the stage for a long line of models predicated on its enduring design. Later models had wing-tip floats and the PBY-5A was an amphibian with wheels folding up into the sides of the hull. During the war, the aircraft served in many capacities, but perhaps none was more valuable than as a search-and-rescue platform nicknamed Dumbo.

With the introduction of the PBY-5A in late 1939, the type took on a whole new capability. This model was an amphibian. The newly installed retractable tricycle landing gear provided the ability to operate off either land or water. The US Army Air Forces acquired this model with the OA-10 designation.

In 1941, the Naval Aircraft Factory in Philadelphia brought its expertise to the construction of a redesigned Catalina that included higher gross weight, more fuel, new hull shape, enhanced armament and a taller tail with a horn-balanced rudder. This PBN-1 Nomad, as it was known, represented a major upgrade. The aircraft reached its design zenith when Consolidated opened a new plant to produce an amphibian version of the NAF model. It is estimated that production of all models reached 4,051.

Notable PBY engagements included the sighting on 26 May 1941 of the infamous German battleship *Bismarck* by the crew of an RAF Catalina cruising over a sector of the Atlantic Ocean. The battleship's coordinates were transmitted so that another Catalina could come on station to direct British warships to execute an interception. Also, in the Atlantic persistent surveillance and attack by Catalinas on patrol impeded the underwater stalkers.

Half a world away, in June 1942, a Catalina sighted the Japanese fleet in the vicinity of Midway. Importantly, from late that year and throughout the rest of the war PBYs prowled the Pacific Ocean, often equipped with specialized radar, in sweeps for Japanese vessels. These aircraft were painted a matt black for night operations and were called Black Cats or simply Cats. They carried a host of weapons such as bombs, torpedoes and depth charges.

Mine-laying, convoy escort and long-range transport are among the additional roles in which the PBY thrived during its many years of service. But perhaps the type's most valuable contribution came in the form of its air-sea rescues. In this role, the PBY was nicknamed Dumbo after the friendly flying elephant in Walt Disney cartoons. Many American airmen downed in combat and floating helplessly at sea owed their lives to these aircraft and their heroic crews that would swoop down and pluck them out of the water.

Specifications (for PBY-5A)
Manufacturer: Consolidated Aircraft
Type: patrol bomber amphibian with crew of seven to nine
Powerplant: two 1,200-horsepower Pratt & Whitney R-1830-92 Twin Wasp radial piston engines
Wingspan: 104 ft 0 in
Length: 63 ft 10 in
Height: 20 ft 2 in
Maximum take-off weight: 35,420 lb
Maximum speed: 175 miles per hour
Cruising speed: 113 miles per hour (on patrol)
Service ceiling: 21,600 ft
Range: 2,350 miles
Armament: one 0.5-in machine gun in each waist blister, one or two 0.3-in machine gun(s) in bow turret, one 0.3-in machine gun in rear ventral position, four depth charges and two torpedoes or four 1,000-lb bombs on separate racks under the wing

Wooden Wonder: De Havilland Mosquito
Generally regarded as one of the greatest military aircraft ever built, the Mosquito was noteworthy for its versatility, speed and construction. As often happens with unconventional design concepts, the Mosquito was at first given short shrift from government officials. The idea of a bomber constructed of wood and bereft of defensive armament made procurement officers blanch. It was the undying faith of company executives, including founder Geoffrey de Havilland, that kept the project alive until finally the RAF approved it in January 1940.

During the hair-raising summer of that year, the Mosquito came close to extinction on a couple of occasions before construction of the first one could even be completed. But each time it looked as if the project would be sacrificed on the bureaucratic altar, the venture was resuscitated. The aircraft that was conceived in 1938 as an internal company project launched into the air for the first time at de Havilland's Hatfield headquarters on 25 November 1940. Once in flight, the RAF finally could see the value in this uncommon platform.

A factor that intervened to improve the concept's viability was the spread of the shooting war over the homeland only a few months before which impelled the authorities to select a wooden aircraft given that wartime supplies of strategic metals were bound to dwindle. The Mosquito's wood construction was of a plywood/balsa/plywood sandwich layering. Advantages included light weight and strength. The wood was pressed and bonded into the requisite shapes with smooth outer surfaces that enhanced the aerodynamic contour.

The aircraft had a relatively slender fuselage with increased taper in the tail section. The mid-wing's trailing edge was swept forward. Two Rolls-Royce Merlin engines were fitted in wing-mounted nacelles into which the main landing gear retracted. The two-man crew sat side-by-side under an expansive framed glass canopy.

The svelte frontal cross-section and powerful engines enabled impressive climb and speed performance. With a maximum speed for most models of nearly 400 miles per hour, the Mosquito could outrun some *Luftwaffe* fighters. Also, later models had a pressurized cabin that allowed flight at very high altitudes, making it hard for fighters to keep up the chase.

The Mosquito's lean profile and wood construction represented an early form of stealth. The fact that the Mosquito posted a loss rate of only 0.7 per cent, the lowest of any British bomber during the war, says much about the type's survivability. To the *Luftwaffe*'s continuing frustration, the Mosquito operated with virtual impunity.

This bomber variant of the Mosquito in the RAF's No. 15 Squadron participated in the successful low-level mission against the Phillips electronics plant in Eindhoven, the Netherlands, on 6 December 1942. The same squadron had been the first to conduct a bombing raid in the Mosquito B.Mk IV earlier in the year.

In September 1941, an unarmed Mosquito PR.Mk I flew a photo-reconnaissance mission along the French coast, representing the type's initial combat service. The next May, No. 105 Squadron flew the first bombing mission in the Mosquito B.Mk IV. That same month, the Mosquito NF.Mk III entered the fray as a night fighter equipped with four 20-mm cannon and four 0.303-in machine guns. The various models excelled in their different roles, proving the extent of the Mosquito's adaptability.

The Mosquito B.Mk IX had an enlarged bomb bay which could carry a 4,000-pound bomb. This variant was also equipped with the 'Oboe' pathfinding radar to lead RAF heavy bombers to their night bombing targets. An anti-shipping version, the Mosquito FB.Mk XVIII, carried a 57-mm Molins gun internally that fired six-pound shells. Additionally, Mosquitoes were all-purpose fighter/bombers, minelayers, trainers, and high-speed transports.

Pinpoint strikes were in the Mosquito's repertoire, too. On 25 September 1942, the *Gestapo* headquarters in Oslo was attacked and the occupiers' records of the Norwegian resistance fighters were destroyed. In one of the war's most daring raids, Mosquitoes strafed the prison at Amiens, north of Paris, shattering the walls so that some of the interned resistance fighters could escape.

US Army Air Forces squadrons flew the light bomber and photo-reconnaissance Mosquitoes. Some of the American-flown Mosquitoes were used to dispense chaff in advance of bomber formations as a way to trick German radar. An American special operations squadron, flying the Mosquito PR.Mk XVI, conducted surreptitious missions in support of resistance fighters.

The Mosquito was affectionately nicknamed the 'Wooden Wonder' and the 'Mossie'. From serious doubts about its practicality which almost sank it before it ever got off the ground, this brilliantly conceived aircraft achieved immortality. Mosquito production totalled 7,781, including aircraft built in Canada and Australia.

Specifications (for Mk IV)
Manufacturer: de Havilland Aircraft
Type: two-seat light bomber
Powerplant: two 1,250-horsepower Rolls-Royce Merlin XXI liquid-cooled V-12 engines
Wingspan: 54 ft 3 in
Length: 40 ft 10 in
Height: 15 ft 3 in
Maximum take-off weight: 21,823 lb
Maximum speed: 380 miles per hour
Cruising speed: 255 miles per hour
Service ceiling: 31,082 ft
Range: 1,219 miles
Armament: up to 2,000 lb of bombs

Chapter 5

Supplying through the Sky: Transports

To a large extent, the winning aircraft of World War II were designed and developed either just before the outbreak of hostilities or shortly after the war began. Also, these aircraft were conceived from the outset as military platforms to be wielded as instruments of air power. Exceptions were few and far between, none more prominent than the twin-engine Douglas civil airliner that was transformed into a mainstay of the Allies' cargo and troop transport operations.

On 17 December 1935, the thirty-second anniversary of the Wright brothers' success at Kitty Hawk, the Douglas DC-3 rose from Clover Field in Santa Monica, California, on its maiden flight. Little could the Douglas Aircraft design team, including company founder Donald W. Douglas, have known then that their creation would not only revolutionize commercial air travel but also give the Allied forces a distinct advantage over their Axis foes in the coming war.

Indeed, after the war, General Dwight Eisenhower opined that the majority of senior officers considered the militarized version of the Douglas transport to be among the four pieces of equipment most important to winning the war in Africa and Europe. The others were the bulldozer, Jeep, and 2½-ton truck, none of which, curiously enough, was designed for use in warfare.

The almost instant success of the DC-3, which enabled the airlines to turn a profit for the first time without reliance on airmail contracts, drew the interest of the US Army Air Corps. The aircraft's impressive performance was owed to the specifications laid down for the DC-3's precursor by Transcontinental & Western Air in a letter of 2 August 1932. The letter called for the new Douglas airliner, the DC-1, to be able to take off with one engine inoperable from the airport with the highest field elevation on the airline's cross-country route. Donald Douglas referred to this requirement as the 'birth certificate of the modern airliner'. The requirement was later changed to include the ability to climb on a single engine above the route's mountain peaks.

With a pre-war civilian gross weight certification of 25,200 pounds and the capacity to carry twenty-one passengers, the DC-3 represented an excellent 'off-the-shelf' military transport, subject, of course, to modification for cargo and troops. The aircraft was rugged, too. Airlines were discovering that even when severe turbulence struck or mid-air collisions occurred with chunks of the wings sheared off, the aircraft usually forged ahead.

Perhaps the best example of the type's durability was illustrated by an incident in the summer of 1941. The starboard wing of a parked China National Airways Corporation

DC-3 sustained major damage during a Japanese air assault. Only a DC-2 wing was available as a replacement. Though five feet shorter than the DC-3 wing, it was installed and, according to reports, 'the airliner flew splendidly.' Under the circumstances, 'this aircraft was christened the DC-2½.'

By the time America entered World War II, 507 DC-3s had been produced, of which 434 went to commercial operators. A total of 289 were being flown by US airlines. Soon, production of military versions would eclipse the prior civil airliner output. Douglas was impelled to supplement its Santa Monica operation by establishing new factories at Long Beach, California, and Oklahoma City, Oklahoma. By mid-1944, the company was completing a C-47 and similar military variants at the rate of one every thirty-four minutes.

When war erupted and the Allies needed a general-purpose transport, it was fortunate that the DC-3 was there. In its C-47 military designation, it proved to be an exceptionally capable and adaptable aircraft, a true wartime workhorse. The crews who flew the aircraft showered the type with praise.

Other transports besides the C-47 provided valuable service, too. Douglas produced the C-54 Skymaster based on its four-engine DC-4 airliner. The C-54 was bigger than the C-47. It also had a longer range. The first production model flew in early 1942, but only 1,242 were built. Notably, the first dedicated Presidential transport was a modified C-54A named the *Sacred Cow*. It was equipped with an electric lift in the tail section to accommodate President Franklin Roosevelt in his wheelchair.

The Curtiss C-46 Commando was the remaining major transport aircraft operated by the US during the war. The first C-46 was delivered to the Army Air Forces in the summer of 1942. Because of its long range and double-lobe fuselage which gave it a greater load capacity than the C-47, the type was used mainly in the Far East. The C-46 developed a deserved reputation for sustaining the Allied effort in China by flying with regularity over the hazard-laden 'Hump'.

Though the supply function has often been neglected in warfare, the more astute commanders have recognized it as essential to victory. The pilots and crews of the transports are not typically in the forefront of air combat histories, but without their service those at the tip of the spear could hardly survive let alone triumph.

Sometimes the transports had to run the gauntlet of enemy fire and they generally lacked armament with which to shoot back. Airfield conditions and the operating environments were frequently anathema to flight, yet the transport crews had a job to do and they performed it in spite of the ominous peril. The contributions of the transport crews were no less heroic than those of their fighter and bomber counterparts.

Hump Hurdler: Curtiss C-46 Commando

The C-46 originated from a Curtiss-Wright airliner concept meant to compete with the *sine qua non* of the airliners of the 1930s, the standard-setting Douglas DC-3. Curtiss had a presence in the commercial airliner business, but by the mid-1930s its lumbering Condor was clearly antiquated and being surpassed by all-metal monoplanes from Lockheed, Boeing and the aforementioned Douglas. To keep up with the other companies, Curtiss designed the Model CW-20, which was larger with a bigger payload capacity, though it was, like the competitors, a taildragger configuration powered by twin radial engines.

A sense of the load capacity of the C-46 is evident in this image of troops boarding through the port cargo door. The C-46 had a voluminous cabin because of its two-lobe configuration. Its flights 'over the Hump' between India and China were noteworthy.

Designed to carry thirty-six passengers, the US Army Air Corps saw the potential for a cargo/transport version. This made sense since the Curtiss design was stockier and, at least in theory, could carry a heavier load than the first-generation of twin-engine, all-metal airliners which already operated on commercial routes. The CW-20's extra cabin capacity came from the fact that its fuselage was configured as two circular sections, sometimes called lobes, joined longitudinally.

To smooth over the crease at this longitudinal joint, a fairing was inserted. But the fill-in cover did not provide any performance improvement, so it was removed. The windscreen and cockpit side windows were flush with the nose, a fairly distinctive design feature that made the type instantly recognizable. A batch of C-46B production units had a more traditional stepped windscreen, but the manufacturer returned to making its original nose in the C-46D, which was distinguishable from earlier models in that it had double cargo doors. The windscreen changes occurred again between the E and F models.

In the spring of 1940, the prototype's twin-finned tail proved to be inefficient in flight testing. The solution came in the adoption of a more conventional single fin/rudder arrangement. On 21 June 1941, the US Army bought the subsequent test article, which it designated the C-55. After three months of further evaluation, the aircraft was sold to a foreign airline.

These C-46As are depicted in an all-metal finish and a painted finish. By mid-1944, it was decided to forgo the painted exterior. Doing so saved money and time. An additional benefit was increased speed because of the reduction in weight.

The C-46 production models, which had been ordered in quantity in September 1940, would utilize the C-55 tail design. First deliveries began to arrive on 12 July 1942. Soon, the transport was modified with a cargo door in the aft port fuselage to accommodate oversize equipment like big aircraft engines, Jeeps and supplies stacked on pallets. Nicknamed the Commando, the aircraft could haul up to forty fully equipped troops.

C-46s served in many theatres during World War II, but they were used most extensively in Asia where their greater load-carrying ability was desperately needed to supply American and Chinese forces confronting the diffuse Japanese presence. It was in the China-Burma-India area of operations that the type established its enduring reputation as an indispensable component in the do-or-die lifeline to Chunking, the principal destination where supplies were offloaded.

Negotiating the unforgiving terrain of the Himalayan range, barely clearing craggy bluffs at 14,000 feet in adverse weather with a full load of flammable aviation fuel, required nerves of steel. The transport pilots and crew persevered to keep the air bridge open. The experience gave rise to the expression 'flying over the Hump'.

The type was employed as a troop carrier in Europe and a small number went to the Marine Corps as the R5C-1. The aircraft remained in US Air Force service for years to come, albeit in declining numbers. Its last notable role, eminently appropriate for an aircraft called the Commando, was during the Vietnam War as a counterinsurgency platform with the famed 1st Air Commando Wing.

Specifications (for C-46A)
Manufacturer: Curtiss-Wright
Type: troop/cargo transport with a typical crew of four
Powerplant: two 2,000-horsepower Pratt & Whitney R-2800-51 Double Wasp 18-cylinder radial piston engines
Wingspan: 108 ft 1 in
Length: 76 ft 4 in
Height: 21 ft 9 in
Maximum take-off weight: 56,000 lb
Maximum speed: 269 miles per hour
Cruising speed: 183 miles per hour
Service ceiling: 27,600 ft
Range: 1,200 miles
Load: cargo of 10,000 lb or fifty troops or thirty-three litters and four medics

Old Reliable: Douglas C-47 Skytrain
Donald Douglas and his talented team of designers could hardly have imagined in the mid-1930s as they put the finishing touches on the DST (Douglas Sleeper Transport), the third in a new family of commercial airliners, that with relatively minor modification the aircraft would become the most widely used transport in the looming war or that it would emerge as a shining symbol of freedom's triumph over tyranny. The step toward glory occurred when American Airlines asked Douglas Aircraft for a bigger version of its existing all-metal twin, the DC-2. The new airliner would have to accommodate fourteen passengers with sleeping berths and provide the safety of single-engine performance should one of the two engines quit.

The Army Air Corps took delivery of its first Douglas DC-3 on 14 September 1939. It was designated the C-41A. That aircraft, pictured here, was used initially as the transport for Secretary of War Henry Stimson and later as a regular staff transport. The highly successful DC-3 airliner was the basis for the US Army's C-47 and the US Navy's R4D. These cargo/troop transports were among the most important aircraft of the war.

Because there wasn't much demand for berths, Douglas converted the cabin for day operations, installing twenty-one passenger seats. This modified DST became the DC-3. When the airliner started plying commercial routes in 1936, it caught the attention of other airlines which were mindful of the aircraft's advantages. Within three years, more than 90 per cent of US airline passengers flew on the type or its smaller predecessor, the DC-2.

The US Army Air Corps had tracked the development of the family of Douglas twin-engine airliners and, in July 1936, bought some DC-2s. With the introduction of the bigger DC-3 around that time, the US Army saw the value in a militarized version of the new Douglas design. As need for that type of aircraft grew, Douglas got word that an Army version would have to have more powerful engines, a reinforced floor and a strengthened tail section to accommodate a cargo door.

First production deliveries of the C-47 occurred in 1941, but these arrived at a crawling pace because of the company's strained assembly line capacity and start-up adjustments at a new plant. Because of its urgent need for transports, the US Army requisitioned many existing civil DC-3s. A priority was placed on ramping up the military transport's production rate.

After the baseline C-47 production model, the company made the C-47A, which contrasted with the forerunner by having a higher voltage electrical system. The RAF began to take significant deliveries of the A model, known in RAF parlance as the Dakota Mk III. This moniker differed markedly from the prosaic official US name of Skytrain. The remaining major production model was the C-47B, which had two-stage superchargers to improve high-altitude performance for the China supply route over treacherous mountain ridges.

The C-47's success had much to do with the simplicity of its design. A stressed-skin aircraft made of light alloy and with a low cantilevered wing, it was a sturdy structure, destined in some cases to last for many decades. A nearly circular fuselage enabled carriage of wide and tall loads. Because of a decent thrust-to-weight ratio the transport had a payload capacity of 6,000 pounds.

The modern equipment that went into the construction of the C-47 was, by and large, readily available from suppliers, which meant that proven technologies like pneumatic wing de-icing boots, hydraulically operated split-type flaps, cowl flaps and constant-speed propellers ensured reliable operation. During the war and long afterwards, C-47 pilots and crew praised the transport, often remarking that the aircraft gave them an extra margin of performance, providing a little more in the way of climb and cruise in tight spots when those attributes were sorely needed.

The type's most memorable service came on 6 June 1944 when a total of over 1,000 C-47s participated in the D-Day invasion, the long-anticipated Allied offensive to liberate continental Europe. Some carried paratroopers while others towed gliders which carried yet more troops. Many of the more than 24,000 Allied soldiers who were flown to the battle arrived via these transports.

In fact, a version of the C-47 was made expressly for the paratroop mission. Designated the C-53 Skytrooper, this model abandoned the hardened floor and oversize cargo doors. Instead, its cabin was lined with seats for twenty-eight paratroopers.

The US Navy's equivalent of the Army's Air Transport Command was the Naval Air Transport Service, which operated about 600 C-47s with the designation R4D followed by the pertinent model number. During the war, US production of the C-47 totalled 10,048. An estimated 2,700 were built in the Soviet Union as the Lisunov Li-2. About 500 were constructed by Japan and coded 'Tabby' by the Allies.

After World War II, the C-47 continued in Air Force service for many years, notably during the Berlin Airlift, delivering vital supplies to break the Soviet blockade, and during the Vietnam War as the AC-47 gunship, which was known as *Puff the Magic Dragon*. Other variants have remained in civil operation, hauling freight, servicing skydivers at jump schools and giving scenic aerial tours. Some have even undergone turboprop conversions.

The type has outlasted virtually all the military transports that have been introduced since it first flew in Air Corps livery. The Gooney Bird's predominant virtue was that it came through when needed. Flight crews could count on the pre-war airliner, modified for military service, to finish the mission and get them home safely.

Specifications (for C-47A)
Manufacturer: Douglas Aircraft
Type: troop/cargo transport and glider tug with a typical crew of three
Powerplant: two 1,200-horsepower Pratt & Whitney R-1830-93 Twin Wasp radial piston engines
Wingspan: 95 ft 0 in
Length: 64 ft 2 in
Height: 16 ft 11 in
Maximum take-off weight: 26,000 lb
Maximum speed: 229 miles per hour
Cruising speed: 185 miles per hour
Service ceiling: 23,200 ft
Range: 1,500 miles
Load: cargo of 10,000 lb or 28 troops or 18 litters

Author

Philip Handleman is the President of Handleman Filmworks, an independent production company that has produced award-winning public television documentaries on the Holocaust, the Vietnam War and other subjects. Mr Handleman's still photography has been featured on US postage stamps, including his image of the Thunderbirds air demonstration team on the 1997 commemorative stamp honouring the fiftieth anniversary of the US Air Force and his image of the Cadet Chapel on the 2004 commemorative stamp honouring the fiftieth anniversary of the US Air Force Academy.

In addition, Mr Handleman has been an active private pilot for thirty-nine years and currently owns and flies two aircraft of military lineage, including an open-cockpit biplane of World War II vintage. Mr Handleman's deep attachment to the world of flight is reflected in the more than seventy aviation articles and the twenty-one aviation books he has written.

A tireless champion of aeronautics, he successfully fought a landmark legal case that defined the limits of municipal control over airport flight activity. Additionally, he fostered regulatory protections for users of the US airspace system. Also, in June 2002, he initiated the effort to secure legislation to recognize the legendary Tuskegee Airmen with the award of the Congressional Gold Medal, which occurred on 29 March 2007. Mr Handleman's first flight instructor was a Tuskegee Airman.

Mr Handleman is a long-time trustee of the Michigan Air Guard Historical Association, which oversees the state's largest military air museum. In 2008, he received the Harriet Quimby Award from the Michigan Aviation Hall of Fame for contributions to aviation art and literature. In 2010, he received the Combs Gates Award from the National Aviation Hall of Fame for his contributions to the preservation of America's air and space heritage.

Mr Handleman received a bachelor's degree from Washington University and afterwards pursued post-graduate studies at the University of Michigan's Graduate School of Business Administration. He and his wife, Mary, divide their time between their home in suburban Detroit and a private airstrip in the nearby countryside.